Derbyshire
Edited by Steve Twelvetree

First published in Great Britain in 2004 by:
Young Writers
Remus House
Coltsfoot Drive
Peterborough
PE2 9JX
Telephone: 01733 890066
Website: www.youngwriters.co.uk

All Rights Reserved

© *Copyright Contributors 2004*

SB ISBN 1 84460 490 X

Foreword

Young Writers was established in 1991 and has been passionately devoted to the promotion of reading and writing in children and young adults ever since. The quest continues today. Young Writers remains as committed to engendering the fostering of burgeoning poetic and literary talent as ever.

This year's Young Writers competition has proven as vibrant and dynamic as ever and we are delighted to present a showcase of the best poetry from across the UK. Each poem has been carefully selected from a wealth of *Once Upon A Rhyme* entries before ultimately being published in this, our twelfth primary school poetry series.

Once again, we have been supremely impressed by the overall high quality of the entries we have received. The imagination, energy and creativity which has gone into each young writer's entry made choosing the best poems a challenging and often difficult but ultimately hugely rewarding task - the general high standard of the work submitted amply vindicating this opportunity to bring their poetry to a larger appreciative audience.

We sincerely hope you are pleased with our final selection and that you will enjoy *Once Upon A Rhyme Derbyshire* for many years to come.

Contents

Eleanor Hanmer (11)   1

All Saints CE Junior School
Emma Erskine (9)   1
Michael Green (8)   2
Molly Reeve (7)   2
Emily Thoday (9)   3
Courtney Andrews (8)   3
Tony Elkington (8)   4
Michael Squires (8)   5
Benjamin Haynes (8)   6
Harris Lovatt (8)   6
Jack Beers (8)   7
Katie Watkinson (8)   7
Harry Spencer (8)   8
Kieran Taylor (8)   8
Sophie Grindrod (7)   8
Thomas Parkin (8)   9
Abbie Skinner Biring (7)   9
Nicola Rimmer (8)   9
Tristan Kawalek (8)   10
Louise Smith (9)   10
Rebecca Rimmer (8)   10
Laura Wainwright (9)   11
Zak Cooper (7)   11
James Jenkins (9)   12

Apperknowle Primary School
Emily Savage (10)   13
Jade Lee (9)   13
Faye Baggaley (10)   14
Jessica Timms (8)   14
Rebecca Carr-Smith (10)   15
Martin Chedgey (9)   15
Chloe Grayson (11)   16
Bradley Thomas (7)   16

Bamford Primary School

Alex Harman (11)	17
Alex Miller (8)	17
Alice Shaw (7)	18
Bluebell Evans (9)	18
Ellice Botham (10)	18
Nicola Harrold (8)	19
Charlotte Hallam (9)	19
Louise Holtum (9)	19
Nina Handley (10)	20
Hannah Towers (9)	20
Sophie Maltby (9)	21
Oliver Cooper (10)	21
Philippa Betts-Dawson (8)	22
Laura Crookes (9)	22
Jessica Hawley (8)	22
Gabrielle Gillott (8)	23
Jessica Leng (8)	23
Edward Selvey (8)	23
Jessica Lindley (7)	24
Alexander Coates (10)	24
Katie Hodges (11)	25
Beth Keable (8)	26

Chapel-en-le-Frith Primary School

Jenny Hague (9)	26
Thomas Theyer (8)	27
Samuel Lee (8)	27
James Whitehead (8)	28
Tyler Byatte (8)	28
Jessica Lomas (8)	29
Francis Oakes (9)	29
Sinéad Hammond (9)	30
Chloe Hall (8)	31
Sarah Coe	32
Sarah Critchlow (9)	32
Mollie Rowland (9)	33
Aaron Sharp (9)	33
Mark Watson (9)	34
Timothy Greenhalgh (9)	34
Hannah Mycock (8)	35

Matthew Green (9)	35
David Twaites (8)	36
Sam Hesketh	36
Bethanie Williamson (9)	36

Denby Free CE (Aided) Primary School

Jack Shepperd (11)	37
Hannah Glenn (9)	37
Matthew Manley (9)	37
Charlotte Richardson (10)	38
Alex Taylor (10)	38
Chloe Barlow (9)	39
Daniel Middleton (10)	40
Jody Crooks (11)	40
Daniel Sarson (11)	41
Emily Allsop (10)	41
Shannon Jarvis (9)	42
Lucy Mellor (9)	42
Madeleine Walker (10)	43
Jack Lawrence (11)	44

Granby Junior School

Bronwyn Stevens (10)	45
Jemma Browning (8)	45
Paige Bailey (8)	46
Kyle Scott (10)	46
Sophie Barratt (8)	47
Anya Holland (8)	47
Emily Tindall (8)	48
Louise Priest (9)	48
Cally Smith (8)	49
Amber Shanahan (10)	49
Natalie Brown (10)	50
Demi Drew (9)	50
Kirby Edwards (8)	51
Lucy Graham (10)	51
Charlotte Heseltine (9)	52
Chloe Wood (11)	52
Olivia Gibson (10)	52
Matthew Ashley (11)	53
Francessca Wilcock (9)	53

Emily Buck (10)	53
Carly Baker (9)	54
Chloe Rachel Foulkes (8)	54
Nikita Stevenson (8)	54
Holly Bramley (10)	55
Jackie Spencer (8)	55
Abigail Sisson (9)	55
Amy Brooks (9)	56
Laurie Plant (8)	56
Amy Lockwood (9)	56

Grindleford Primary School

Rebecca Baraona (10)	57
Ruth Jackson (8)	57
David Gill (9)	58
George Wrench (8)	58
Joanne Barber (9)	58
Jack Maynard (9)	59
Harry William Bushell (11)	59
William Gratton (9)	59
Freddie Thomas Reynolds (10)	60
Holly Ragdale (11)	60
Sam Willis (11)	60
Rebecca Bowman (11)	61
Robbie Jackson (9)	61
Beth Willis (9)	61
Charlie Bushell (9)	62
Meryn Norman (9)	62
Liam Friend (10)	62
Craig Wilson (11)	63
Josh Cadman (10)	63

Hardwick Junior School

Ali Chaudhry (9)	64
Selina Hussain (10)	65
Maimuna Saliha (10)	65
Stacy Ann Shepherd (10)	66
Marcus Ward (10)	66
Jade Jessica Weeks (10)	67
Oliver Jacob Culley de Lange (9)	67
Zoheb Hussain (10)	68

Mandeep Singh Sangha (9)   68
Poppy Sephton Clark (9)   68
Mubasher Sajid (10)   69
Adam Brown (9)   69

Hartsthorne CE Primary School
Shelly Wilkinson   70
Amy Jenkinson (9)   70
Rebecca Redfern (10)   71
Romany Freeman (9)   71
William Alexander (11)   72
George Fletcher (10)   72
Alex Patrick (9)   73

Measham CE Primary School
Catherine Timbrell (10)   73
Lucy Lakin (11)   74
Adora Mottram (7)   74
Jordan Haynes (11)   75
Georgia Banton (9)   75
Anna Aldersley (10)   76
Christopher Fisher (11)   76
Lauren Mason (10)   77
Kyle Sanders (11)   77
Josh Grascia (10)   78
Emma Roach (11)   78
Ashleigh McClane-Smith (10)   79
Victoria Ince (11)   79
Ben Thompson (10)   80
Bethany Coleman (11)   80
Yasmin Tills (10)   81
Michaela Smeaton (10)   81
Loretta Hull (10)   82
Parris Wileman (11)   82
Grace Noble (10)   83
Leah Brown (11)   83
Abbey Lish (9)   84
Thomas Patrick (11)   84
Reiss Fielding (11)   85
Adam Hollens (10)   85
Jonathan Cobb (10)   86

Lauren Surch (11) — 87
Ellie Cashmore (11) — 88
Hannah Bourne (10) — 88

Mickleover Primary School

Rhiannon Smallman (8) — 89
Daniel Beddow (8) — 89
Leonie King (9) — 90
Thomas Robson (8) — 90
Alex Scrivener (9) — 91
Emily Reader (8) — 91
Georgie Barker (9) — 92
Alexander James Suckling (8) — 92
Emma Shaw (9) — 93
Sam Aulsebrook (9) — 93
Thomas Fletcher (8) — 94
Alexandra Jayne Nelson (8) — 94
Harriet McDonnell (9) — 94
Jamie Turner (9) — 95
Helen Perry (8) — 95
Natasha Payne (9) — 95
Hannah Wagg (8) — 96
Chris Mann (9) — 96
Ryan Skidmore (9) — 96
Daniel Harrison (8) — 97
Lydia Roworth (8) — 97
Katie Yeomans (8) — 97
Laurie-Leigh Grainger (8) — 98
Luke Cheetham (8) — 98
Danny Cunningham (8) — 99
Jessica Burman (9) — 99
Amelia Draper (10) — 100
Evangeline Harvie (10) — 101
Edward Ody (9) — 102
Emma Swindell (10) — 103
Tom Foster (8) — 103
Lewis Thomas (10) — 104
Bethan Crocker (9) — 105
Jenna Dunn (9) — 106
Ellie Joslin (10) — 107
May Worthington (9) — 108

Megan Aubeeluck-Davies (9)	109
Sam Forrest (9)	110
Alex Brannan (10)	111
Natasha Bugg (10)	112
Coral Hancox (9)	113
Lucy Atkinson (10)	114
Lucy Elliott (10)	115
Dominique Grocott (10)	116
George Hall (10)	117
Josh Gahonia (9)	118
Ben Clarke (9)	119
Steven Cornforth (10)	120
Siân Grant (9)	121
Susannah Barnard (9)	122
Nicole Dunn (9)	123
Jack Pritchard (10)	124
Alec James (9)	124

Redhill Primary School

Nicholas Reed (10)	125
Sophie Webster (9)	125
Vanessa Radford (10)	126
Haydn Bowley (9)	126
George Cant (9)	127
Kirsty Dakin (9)	127
Amelia Fletcher-Jones (9)	128
Tristan Foster (9)	128
Laura Clough (10)	129
Vanessa Emery (10)	129
Holly-Robyn Hempell (7)	130
Jamie Fenwick (10)	130
Alex Miskow (9)	131
Coral Fitzhugh (9)	131
Jonathan Hatchett (10)	131
Thomas Reed (7)	132
Katie Levers (8)	132
Brendan Hewitson (8)	132
Hayley Sherlock (7)	133
Thomas Morgan (8)	133
Henry Sharpe (7)	133
Jason McKenzie (8)	134

Alex Woods (8)	134
Alex Brown (7)	135
Eleanor Parry (8)	135
Hannah Sisson (7)	136
Thomas Galloway (7)	136
Benjamin Tennett (7)	136
Isabel Walters (7)	137
Vicky Horton (11)	137
Emma Little (10)	137
Jade McKenzie (10)	138
Susan Frankish (11)	138
Theodora Maguire (10)	138
Ashley Smith (10)	139
James McKinnon (11)	139
Rosie Hunter (11)	139
Abigail Teflise (11)	140
Tom Mills (10)	140
Alex Baldwin (11)	140
Jenny Jones (8)	141
Connor Hewitson (10)	141
Shayne White (10)	142

St George's CE Primary School, High Peak

Brogan Brown (10)	142
Joseph Ingham (11)	143
Joshua Clinton (9)	143
Natasha Spencer (10)	144
Leanne Williamson (10)	144
Megan Chatterton (10)	145
Halana Mellor (11)	145
Hollie Maxwell (11)	146
Ryan Williams (10)	146
Chloe Barton (11)	146
Andrew Wood (10)	147

St Peter & St Paul School, Chesterfield

Tom Brown (9)	147
Alexander Hodgkinson (8)	147
Becky Hartshorn (9)	148
Callum Howie (9)	148
Richard Berry (8)	148

Laura Singleton (8)	149
Bryony Price (9)	149
Edward Richardson (8)	149
Suzannah Hayes (9)	150
James Davies (9)	150
Sabah Jadoon (9)	151
Ryan Hinchliffe (9)	151
Katherine Parkin (9)	152
Amber Richardson (8)	152
Lewis Spencer (9)	152
Charlotte Thompson (9)	153
James Sharpe (8)	153
Katie Patrick (8)	153
Bethanie Twigg (9)	154
Rowan Borchers (9)	154
Rebecca Bayliff (8)	155
Siân Carter (8)	155
Gagan Shiralagi (7)	156
Laura Hattersley (9)	156
Charlotte Adams (9)	156

St Werburgh's CE Primary School, Spondon

Beth Wood (10)	157
Christina-Mary Wilford (10)	157
Lucy Siena (11)	157
Jade Hogan (11)	158
Ben Osborn (9)	158
Joseph Cunningham (10)	159
Sophie Ford (9)	159
Catherine Harper (10)	160
Terry Ashley (11)	160
Bethan Hall (9)	161
Charlotte Eastwood (10)	161
Jessica Holyoake (10)	162
Luke Sumpter (10)	162
Nicol Winfield (11)	163
Rebecca Bonsall (10)	163
Thomas Cornfield (11)	164
Emma Newman (10)	164
Mark Harrison (9)	164

Rachel Evans (11) — 165
Paige Bray (10) — 165

St Wystan's School, Repton
Matthew Cort (10) — 166
Callum McLean (9) — 166
Thomas Jones (10) — 167
Robert Egan (10) — 167
Jessica Storey (9) — 168
Aimee Holder-Spinks (9) — 168
Sophie Donoghue (10) — 169
Oliver Richards (9) — 169
David Chandler (10) — 170
Holly Twells (10) — 171
William Barnett (9) — 172
Emily Hammond (10) — 173
Richard Gidlow (9) — 174
Victor Scattergood (10) — 175
Tristan Griffiths (9) — 176
Benedict Cross (9) — 177

South Darley CE Primary School
Naomi Dodds (11) — 177
Holly Ibbotson (9) — 178
Emily Rathbone (10) — 179
Ryan McClean (9) — 180
Katherine Holmes (11) — 180
Clare Harrison (10) — 181
Maddy Sixsmith (10) — 181
George Devereaux Evans (10) — 182
Emily Barrow (11) — 182
Daisy Rathbone (9) — 183
Bethany Allwright (9) — 183
Alice Rathbone (10) — 184
Jordan Bullen (9) — 185

Thornsett Primary School
Tom Hardwick-Allan (7) — 185
Max Bradwell (8) — 186
Katrina Cullen (8) — 187

Taylor Jones (9)	188
Chris Williamson (9)	188
Jack Martin (8)	189
Ryan Isted (7)	189
Rory Marshall (7)	190
Hannah Berry (7)	190
Jamie Monkman (10)	191
Sophie Williamson (7)	191
Owen Baldwin (10)	192
Toyah Bradley (11)	192
Iain Barr (8)	193
Poppy Philligreen (8)	193
Katy Waddell (10)	194
Nicola Millard (8)	194
Daisy Whewell (9)	195
Kyle Jones	196
Joe Scholes (10)	196
Hannah Brookes (11)	196

Weston-on-Trent CE (Aided) Primary School

Jacob Walker (11)	197
Leanne Hotter (11)	197
Yasmyn Ford-Paulson (10)	197
Thomas Hamilton (11)	198
Eleanor Dumbill (11)	199
Douglas Brown (10)	200
Laura Poole (10)	200
Luke Perks (11)	201
Charlotte Tyler (11)	201

The Poems

Looking For God

Looking for God where is He now?
Looking for God why can't He be found?
Do we see God through swollen faces
Or bullying of different races?
Do we see God through thunder and lightning
Or through poverty, hunger, war and fighting?
Children suffering, hurting and dying,
Mothers mourn over others wailing and crying.
Third world people ensnared in their own slavery,
Help from the rich countries of the world
. . . Maybe?
Is this the God that we know?
Then what goodness in this world does He show?
We have medicines to save other's lives,
With man's potential not as many die.
Man has walked on the moon,
Now we are waiting for Beagle's arrival soon.
There are still those who kill,
Like he who murdered the 'Soham two'.
Is God's forgiveness and redemption due?
A reminder of a God, a reminder of our mortal existence,
A preparation . . . for our spiritual existence.

Eleanor Hanmer (11)

My Mum

My mum can shout,
My mum can have a drought,
My mum can be kind,
My mum mostly has her own mind.

My mum's meant to be cutting it,
But it's no good, she's still on the wine,
The only problem is there's always something
Wrong with her back or spine!

Emma Erskine (9)
All Saints CE Junior School

Woosh, Neeeow, Bonk!

In the car
driving to the hill
thinking of
woosh, neeeow, bonk!

At the hill
pulling the sledge
thinking of
woosh, neeeow, bonk!

On the top of the hill
getting on the sledge
thinking of
woosh, neeeow, bonk!

Sliding down the hill
crashing into tree
flying over car
woosh, neeeow, bonk!

Michael Green (8)
All Saints CE Junior School

Big Bad Wolf

Pig eater
House beater
Huff puffer
Sneeze snuffer
Bone cruncher
Pork muncher
Bacon cheeker
Wolf sneaker

The big bad wolf!

Molly Reeve (7)
All Saints CE Junior School

Bertie

I have a cat called Bertie
Who thinks she's the boss of me
She thinks she's a tiger
She thinks she's a lion
But she just sits on the settee.

I have a cat called Bertie
Who thinks she's as clever as can be
She thinks she's so fierce
She thinks she's so brave
But she just sits on the settee.

I have a cat called Bertie
Who thinks she could hunt for her tea
She thinks she's so fast
She thinks she's so strong
But she still sits on the settee
(But I think we should have called her Cushion).

Emily Thoday (9)
All Saints CE Junior School

Animal Fun

A nimals are sometimes playful and sometimes sleepy.
N early all the animals are cute and sweet.
I t is important to look after your animal.
M ost animals are sometimes nosy.
A sweet animal normally likes their loves.
L ovely animals they are so fun.

F un, fun that is all animals like,
U sually when cats are kittens they sleep a lot.
N ever let your animal sleep with you, I will tell you,
   you can never get to sleep!

Courtney Andrews (8)
All Saints CE Junior School

Dinosaurs

The T-rex would fill you with fear,
He could, so easily, eat a deer.
He could just fill you full of dread,
He could, as easily, bite off your head!

The tyrannosaurus has two powerful legs,
He always eats meat, but never steals eggs.
He sometimes rushes out, to bite his prey,
If I was you, I'd stay out of his way!

The T-rex can be fifteen metres long,
He surely is amazingly strong.
He definitely is so very mean,
But do not worry, you won't be seen.

The diplodocus is very long,
He surely has the weirdest pong!
He thunders on from foot to foot,
He is, no way, as black as soot.

The diplodocus is as big as a hall,
Wouldn't it help if he was small?
He eats, he eats, he eats all day,
Always leaves, but never hay.

Diplodocus plods from tree to tree,
He really is much bigger than me.
He reaches way up in the sky,
And before I end, he says goodbye.

Tony Elkington (8)
All Saints CE Junior School

The Army

This is the gun
That killed the troop
In the army.

This is the man
That held the gun
That killed the troop
In the army.

This is the tank
That squished the man
That held the gun
That killed the troop
In the army.

This is the plane
That worried the tank
That squished the man
That held the gun
That killed the troop
In the army.

This is the rocket
That followed the plane
That worried the tank
That squished the man
That held the gun
That killed the troop
In the army.

Michael Squires (8)
All Saints CE Junior School

The Mallet The Woodsman Made

Here is the mallet the woodsman made

Here is the minibeasts
That lived in the mallet
The woodsman made.

Here is the woodpecker
That lives on the minibeasts
That lived on the mallet
The woodsman made.

Here is the fox
That ate the woodpecker
That lives on the minibeasts
That lived on the mallet
The woodsman made.

Here is the dinosaur
That devoured the fox
That ate the woodpecker
That lives on the minibeasts
That lived on the mallet
The woodsman made.

Benjamin Haynes (8)
All Saints CE Junior School

Football

F antastic football
O ut in midfield scoring goals
O ffside strikers
T remendous football
B allistic crowds everywhere
A mazing defenders everywhere
L isted players on the board
L osing is bad, winning is good!

Harris Lovatt (8)
All Saints CE Junior School

McLaren

Zoom, zoom, zoom
down the motorway
going 190mph
all the cars zooming behind.
Now going 225mph
'Oops!'

Zoom, zoom, zoom
cops are not as fast
as McLaren.
Helicopters join the chase.

Zoom, zoom, zoom
helicopters are not as fast
as McLaren.
The British Army join the chase.

Zoom, zoom, zoom
McLaren turns a sharp corner
And *bang!*
McLaren gets away.

Jack Beers (8)
All Saints CE Junior School

Snowy Fun

S now is a happy time when you have fun.
N ow it's time to go to school I can't wait, can I catch you?
O h how I love snow, it's really something to look forward to.
W hen we go out to play my brother says, 'Hip, hip . . .'
Y ippee it's time to go home, I can't wait to go sledging.

F irst to have a nice cup of hot chocolate, then the real fun.
U se a nice shovel to build a snowman or woman.
N ow to have a snowball fight, oh no I'm soaked!

Katie Watkinson (8)
All Saints CE Junior School

Snowballs

S nowball fights go on all day
N ever seem to end
O utside on our snowball fighting streets
W hatever the weather snow is the best
B ut when summer comes snow makes a mess
A ll snowballs are cold
L ife is fun when we have snowball fights
L ight is bad for snow.

Harry Spencer (8)
All Saints CE Junior School

I Love Snow

It covers the hills and fields,
It makes me feel quite happy.
The snow is white,
Sometimes bright,
But it always stays in me.

Kieran Taylor (8)
All Saints CE Junior School

Snow

Snow twinkly
Snow sprinkly
Snow fresh
Snow gentle
Snow bright
Snow white.

Sophie Grindrod (7)
All Saints CE Junior School

Football

F ootball is fabulous
O ut in midfield
O ffside and it's a free kick
T remendous sport football
B ad players usually don't score
A mazing goalkeeping
L iverpool are a cool team
L ast half and it's 2-0
   to Liverpool!

Thomas Parkin (8)
All Saints CE Junior School

The Big Snowball

I went outside
All I could see was snow everywhere.
I think I heard my friends' feet
Then a big snowball came rolling down on me
It was my friends
I will never forgive them for it.

Abbie Skinner Biring (7)
All Saints CE Junior School

The Big Bad Wolf Kennings

Bone-cruncher
Animal-muncher
Chimney-climber
Dinner-timer
House-blower
Pig-mower
House-sneaker
Big-weeper.

Nicola Rimmer (8)
All Saints CE Junior School

Skiing

S nowballs flying around
N ow it's time to go
O ver the ski resort to ski
W ith the pro
B eating all the pros
A ll the people shocked
L egs pain
L ike death
S kiing.

Tristan Kawalek (8)
All Saints CE Junior School

My Brother

My brother is annoying,
Especially when he's bonkers!
Zooming round the house.

He eats disgusting things,
Mainly when he's starving.

He normally gets on my nerves,
I wish he was a piece of rock!
All the time!

Louise Smith (9)
All Saints CE Junior School

Snow

S now is the best
N early covered the streets
O n the roads as well
W e hope it will stay.

Rebecca Rimmer (8)
All Saints CE Junior School

The Terrible End

Huffer puffer
Sneezy snuffer.

House blower
Running slower.

Roof hopper
Pork chopper.

Bone cruncher
Pig muncher.

Chimney faller
Getting smaller.

Wolf boiler
Pig spoiler.

Laura Wainwright (9)
All Saints CE Junior School

The Bad Wolf

Teeth clatterer
Pig shatterer

Bone cruncher
Pig muncher

Pig teaser
Pork sizzler

Chimney climber
Sausage timer.

Zak Cooper (7)
All Saints CE Junior School

The Death Of The Duck

Here is the river the man made.

Here is the duck
That swims on the river
The man made.

Here is the lion
That eats the duck
That swims on the river
The man made.

Here are the snakes
That kill the lion
That eats the duck
That swims on the river
The man made.

Here is the T-rex
That gobble the snakes
That kill the lion
That eats the duck
That swims on the river
The man made.

Here is the winter
That wipes out the T-rex
That gobble the snakes
That kill the lion
That eats the duck
That swims on the river
The man made.

James Jenkins (9)
All Saints CE Junior School

Weather

It's always here, it's always rain,
But sun will always come again.

Snow will fall, but soon will go
Spring is here and no more snow.

Sunshine smiling everywhere
And birdies flying through the air.

Cloudy weather, but sun is near,
Hopefully no rain for the rest of the year!

Lightning flashing through the sky,
Electricity's gone but hopes are high.

Bedtime now and sun's gone down,
A beautiful sight all around.

It was a funny day, I can't pretend,
So goodnight to you, and that's . . .

Emily Savage (10)
Apperknowle Primary School

My Friends

Faye is my friend,
She's got a good trend.
Faye likes to play,
All through the day.

Becky is great,
She's my mate.
She's very funny
And she's got a lot of money.

Chloe's got long hair
And she likes her teddy bear.
Chloe is tall,
To her I'm small.

Jade Lee (9)
Apperknowle Primary School

My Friends

Jade is cool,
She acts it at school.
She's very keen,
She's never mean.

Becky is nice,
Perhaps once or twice.
She acts like a fool,
When she is at school!

Jessica is eight,
She's never late.
She always laughs,
And she's good at maths.

Chloe is a dude,
If she's in a good mood.
She likes to play,
On a sunny day.

Faye Baggaley (10)
Apperknowle Primary School

Concorde

C laustrophobic when you're in
O nly have a little grin
N obody knows what it's like
C os I've been on it at night
O n our way I fell asleep
R eally, really, really deep
D ad gave me a poke, 'We're nearly there'
E verybody stopped and stared.

Jessica Timms (8)
Apperknowle Primary School

Stormy Night

As the stormy night grows
The thunder rose
All through the night
Because nothing will go right.

As the waves crashed
The lightning thrashed
The rain came down
Making people frown.

I stand there shivering
As David is complaining
The air is clear
So no more fear!

I tried to make this poem rhyme
Didn't succeed, so never mind!

Rebecca Carr-Smith (10)
Apperknowle Primary School

Sport

My favourite sport is cricket
I always get a wicket!
I bowl nice and straight . . .
But sometimes I hit the garden gate.

When I go in to bat,
I put on my lucky hat.
Can I hit some runs today?
Or surely they won't let me play.

Martin Chedgey (9)
Apperknowle Primary School

Animals

Horses are cute,
Horses are great,
They run around fields,
And jump over gates!

Hamsters may only sleep and eat,
But I still think they're really sweet,
They waddle around in their little cage,
At the moment they're all the rage!

Rabbits like to hop around,
Making such a funny sound,
I have a rabbit called Cheeky,
She's as furry as can be!

Cows moo most of the time,
(I'm having trouble making this rhyme)
If a cow moves away from the herd,
It might tread in a . . . (better not say the word!)

Chloe Grayson (11)
Apperknowle Primary School

Jess Jess

Jess, Jess.
She makes such a mess.
She can head the ball
Even if it hits the wall.
She can head a ball and score a goal
And then head it down a hole.

Bradley Thomas (7)
Apperknowle Primary School

The House Of Horror

I n the house of horrors you will find;
M e, in a state in panic, terrified, and:

G hosts, ghosts, everywhere,
L aughing at me in their evil way,
A ll scary, all haunt me,
D on't like it here at all.

T errifying, horrifying, scarifying for me,
O oooh! They roar, nearly deafening me.

G et away! Go home!
E very one of you, leave me alone!
T his is too scary for me!

O ut! Out! Out! I cry,
U nbelievably frightening,
T errible, terrible place.

Alex Harman (11)
Bamford Primary School

Untitled

I skidded to school on the freezing patch today.
The road was quivery and slimy.
I saw a dog and a man swimming in a freezing lake
I heard a bird and a knight singing and swinging
I felt like ice myself
I rode to school on my bike today
The road was smooth and silky
I saw a bird and people
I heard cars and robins
I felt like the sun myself.

Alex Miller (8)
Bamford Primary School

I Wish It Would Snow . . .

I could build igloos with the frosty snow and the transparent ice.
I could build snowmen and dress them in blue, indigo,
                               silver and gold jackets.
I could have snowball fights and splat my mum and
                               dad with snowballs.
I could go sledging on the sparkling duvet of snow.
I could dance in the snow and pretend to be Odette from Swan Lake.
I wouldn't go to school.
I would watch snowflakes drift and float to the ground.

Alice Shaw (7)
Bamford Primary School

A Week In Smellz

Monday smells of dirty floors and yellow uniform,
Tuesday smells of dust and resin from my bow,
Wednesday smells of gas from just one person!
Thursday smells of scraping from the wall bars in the hall,
Friday smells of chocolate from our secret midnight feast,
Saturday smells of sweets and Black Jacks (they're my fave).
Sunday smells of homework and that's extremely bad!

Bluebell Evans (9)
Bamford Primary School

I Am A River

I am a river, and this is my journey
I twist and twirl
I ebb and curl
And my journey carries on.
I hit some rocks, I spit and spray
And then I travel on my way.
I slip and slide,
And glitter and glide
And then tumble down the weir.

Ellice Botham (10)
Bamford Primary School

Christmas Excitement

I hear bells,
        then footsteps,
and a ho, ho, ho.
        I pretended to be asleep
and I can see a
        big black shadow
and a noise
        like presents being
stuffed in a stocking!

Nicola Harrold (8)
Bamford Primary School

Calipso The Pony

Calipso is beautiful
And a pain in the backside,
Like a dapple-grey rocking horse.
You would love her so much.
'Please be good!'
She bullies all the big ones
by kicking them in the face.
'Oh Calipso,' too late!

Charlotte Hallam (9)
Bamford Primary School

Things I Have Been Doing Lately!

Things I have been doing lately:
Resting on my elbows while watching TV,
Jumping up and down on the settee,
Eating my dinner, scoffing it down,
Biting my fingernails, crick, crack, crick!

Louise Holtum (9)
Bamford Primary School

The River Poem

I form from the rain on the uneven boggy ground,
I dribble slowly forming a trickling sound.

I glitter in the moonlight dancing and prancing,
In the light of the moon.

I bubble, I pound, I bound,
Forming a ferocious sound.

I am a creature of the night,
Nymph of the day, but yet on the Earth I stay.

I am older than the trees,
Younger than you or me.

I gush, I push,
On my never-ending journey!

Nina Handley (10)
Bamford Primary School

Going To Bed

I have to turn on the light for my sister.
Quickly turn on my night light
Before the shadow monster gets my head!
Running down the corridor
Ooh no! The monster's seen me!
Go to the toilet, flush it,
Run out before the toilet monster gets me.
Peg it to my room before the closet monster gets me.
Jump on my bed
Don't move, don't even breathe!
Sucked into its tummy, how gooey!
In the morning, was it a warning?

Hannah Towers (9)
Bamford Primary School

What A Dream

I have to turn the light on for my sister,
Quickly turn my night light on
Before the monster's hand can get my head.
Running down the corridor,
Oh no, he's seen me!
Let's lock the door quick,
Oh no, he's broken it down.
Peg it to my room before the closet monster can get me.
Jump on my bed, don't move, don't even breathe.
Help us, it's coming!
In its tummy, not yummy!
In the morning, what a warning!

Sophie Maltby (9)
Bamford Primary School

In The Night

When winter is bleak and you're asleep
There is a soft sound of creaky floorboards,
Footsteps, the whisper of my mum and dad,
But wait!
Something terrible,
Get under the covers, quick!
Phew! It is my sister!
Rolling and falling out of bed.
Goodnight Mum!
Goodnight Dad!
Love you!
Love you too Oliver.

Oliver Cooper (10)
Bamford Primary School

On A Sunny Day In Summer

Trees swaying in the breeze,
Heather dancing in the wind,
Grass sparkling in the sun and reflecting onto the rocks.
A field full of shimmering grass
Some creamy sheep and a few rustles in the greenness.
The sky starts to fade
The sun is setting
It's the end of the day.

Philippa Betts-Dawson (8)
Bamford Primary School

Horses!

Horses galloping,
    Trotting and prancing,
Proud and tall,
    Tail swishing,
Round and round.
    Ended now,
In his stable,
    Fast asleep,
  Night night.

Laura Crookes (9)
Bamford Primary School

Journey To School

I snowboarded to school
In the snow today,
The road was icy and slippy,
I saw some children
Playing in the snow,
I heard shouting
And a dog barking
I felt wonderful.

Jessica Hawley (8)
Bamford Primary School

Out Of My Window On A Snowy Day In Winter

The icy, crisp, cold sun gently shone down
On the shimmering snow
Snowmen are gazing at me
Icicles hanging
Animals hibernating
Trees swiftly blowing in the breeze
Robins fluttering
Snowflakes shining
Blood-red berries in my mouth
As my lips are cursed with the taste.

Gabrielle Gillott (8)
Bamford Primary School

I Rode To School

I rode to school on a go-kart today
The road was a bit bumpy and steep
I saw a river and a boat
I heard a dog bark and a bird tweet
I felt the air whizz past my hair as I zoomed down a hill.
I rode to school on my horse (Smoky) today
The horse's fur was smooth and warm
I saw a squirrel and a robin
I heard the robin singing
I felt brilliant.

Jessica Leng (8)
Bamford Primary School

Untitled

I glided to school on my sledge today
The road was stiff and skiddy.
I saw some icicles and frozen ponds
I heard cars slithering and children laughing
I felt amazing.

Edward Selvey (8)
Bamford Primary School

The Wood

Down in the wood at the bottom of the road,
There are all sorts of trees young and old.
There are willows and pines at the sides of brooks,
Oaks and elms are homes of rooks.
Mother sparrow's nest keeps her fledglings warm,
Father blue tit digs underground for worms.
Skylark and robin sit high in the trees,
Owl in his dreams sways in the breeze.
Dove preens her feathers in the emerald glade,
Coal tit's pretty feathers have a touch of jade.
Summer days have just begun,
Life in the wood is so much fun!

Jessica Lindley (7)
Bamford Primary School

My Bike

I hate my bike!
It makes small rocks
A mountain hike.

My bike is not very fast,
It's so slow, a tortoise
Could pass.

My brakes are very slow,
I can't stop when I go.

In the bike race
I came last,
Now my bike is in the past!

Alexander Coates (10)
Bamford Primary School

Waterfall

I trickle gently
I dribble under the bridges
I ripple against the rocks
I flow smoothly.
I shimmer as I flow,
I glitter by the swans
I glide freely through the weir
And drift slowly.

I slosh by the fishes
I wallow on my way
I writhe and I bubble
I crash and I crawl.
I splash and I splosh
I slither wavily,
I bound and pounce
I spray as I dance
Waterfall!

I choke and cough
I slip and slide
I splash as I eddy
I spit and I gargle.
I richochet,
I rush,
I wrestle with the rocks
Seasick.

I swirl, I whirl
I twirl, I float
I meander as I curl
I spray, I sing.

I am the River Derwent.
I am the water
On my way to the sea.

Katie Hodges (11)
Bamford Primary School

Journey To School

I ran to school in the rain today
The road was wet and slimy
I saw some cars and a wet cat
I heard a dog barking and the wind singing
I felt brilliant.

I skidded to school in the snow
The road was white and narrow
I saw my friends and a robin
I heard a car beeping and a sheep bleeping
I felt relaxed and cold.

Beth Keable (8)
Bamford Primary School

My Fish Jerry Died Long Ago

My fish Jerry died long ago
He was the love of my life
But some way, somehow he had to go.

He died of fin rot
I cried when he died
I wish he had not.

I was on holiday,
We had a call,
When I was about to play.

Fly away, fly,
My fish's spirit
Fly into the sky.

We laid you in the ground,
Slowly so we would not drop you
And you will never be found.

Jenny Hague (9)
Chapel-en-le-Frith Primary School

I Don't Like What?

I like doing hard work
I don't always like being naughty
I don't like playing games out
I like monsters.

I don't like animals
I like football
I don't like doing coin work
But I like going to school.

I like shouting at my sister
I like my friends
I don't like girls
But I like Disney films.

Thomas Theyer (8)
Chapel-en-le-Frith Primary School

Summer

Summer is hot, summer is fun
It's a lovely sight
Lying on the beach all day
Watching the sun.

Building sandcastles like skyscrapers
Until the tide comes to wash the sand away
To make it soggy just like paper.

When the sun goes down
The sea goes soft.
All the people go back to their houses
And they dream what they would do next year.

Samuel Lee (8)
Chapel-en-le-Frith Primary School

Hallowe'en

It's Hallowe'en. There's screams in the distance.
There's skeletons hung in cages.
Zombies rise from the dead.
The trees are coming alive.

The trees walk everywhere destroying everything in their path.
Trick or treaters are stealing candy.
Evil spirits, ghosts, beasts, walking skeletons.
The horror is being unleashed.

In the wood witches are wandering around the trees
Werewolves are feeding on dead people.
Trees are falling down and people are dying
When they got crushed by the trees.

Pumpkins with scary faces glow in the dark.
They start to come alive.
Headless horsemen ride down the road
Carrying swords killing people as they go.

James Whitehead (8)
Chapel-en-le-Frith Primary School

My Dog Is Silly

My dog is silly because he tries to grab his tail
Then he bangs his head on the door
He doesn't know what he's doing!

He chucks his toys everywhere
He goes out with my mum
He jumps up at my auntie
Even when she isn't feeling very well.

But my dog is stupid.
When he goes back home, he does it all over again.

Tyler Byatte (8)
Chapel-en-le-Frith Primary School

In Summer

In the garden trees sway,
Our rabbit, golden, nibbles
As we play.

Meanwhile my dad loads a pile of leaves,
Busy bees
My sister's new hairstyle.

Growing buds way up high,
Our other rabbit bounces, bouncing away,
Flying birds touch the sky.

Now the bright blue sky drifts away,
A dark grey sky comes today
Autumn is here! Hip hip hooray!
Oh no! It's raining, let's go inside.

Jessica Lomas (8)
Chapel-en-le-Frith Primary School

Have You Seen A Devil?

Have you seen a devil?
Who lives in Hell
On a high level
Whose name is Mell.

With his great red wings,
All he does is slouch
Which means he does not do things,
On the couch!

Have you seen his big red head?
He does not like to see a mouse
He only has a little bed
But in a huge house!

Francis Oakes (9)
Chapel-en-le-Frith Primary School

The Four Seasons

S pring has lots of
P retty flowers and
R ain of spring
I t will bring
N ew life to everything
G ardens will bring up shoots, I'm happy, are you?

S ummer we are in
U p in a plane on holiday
M any exciting things to happen
M um unpacking the suitcase
E veryone's happy and relaxed.
R ushing down to the beach, I'm excited are you?

A utumn gets colder,
U nhappy looks on people's faces,
T rees' leaves fall to the ground.
U nderneath, animals prepare for hibernating
M ore scarves,
N o more shorts. I'm cold are you?

W inter's here
I vy hangs
N ew year is soon
T urkey to get
E veryone's shopping
R eady? I'm ready are you?

Sinéad Hammond (9)
Chapel-en-le-Frith Primary School

The Seasons

S pring's flowers blooming
P laying in the sun.
R unning and jumping
I ce lollies cooling taste
N ice cold food
G oing on holiday.

S ummer's barbecue,
U p comes the sun.
M ornings are so warm
M y suntan
E ntertainment
R iding my bike.

A utumn's leaves begin to fall,
U nderstand the cool days coming,
T elling everybody it's nearly Christmas
U nderstanding the tree's becoming bare
M aking bonfires
N ights getting colder.

W ondering what's for Christmas
I cy lakes so cold
N eeding warmth
T emperature low
E ntertaining Christmas plays
R esting now it's all over.

Chloe Hall (8)
Chapel-en-le-Frith Primary School

My Apostrophe Poem

Best remembered

My cat's big eyes,
My dog's wet tongue,
My mum's mash,
My dad's pancakes,
My brother's piggybacks,
My neighbour's hamster,
My best friend's kindness.

Best forgotten

My dad's mash,
My brother's meanness,
My neighbour's little sister,
My best friend's little sister,
My dad's raspberry blowing,
My dad's music,
My brother's smelly socks.

Sarah Coe
Chapel-en-le-Frith Primary School

Christmas Eve

Christmas Eve is exciting
Because tomorrow is Christmas Day
So everyone shouts, 'Hip hip hooray,'
Because Christmas is on its way.

Sarah Critchlow (9)
Chapel-en-le-Frith Primary School

My Apostrophe Poem

Best remembered

My cat's black fur,
My dog's shiny eyes,
My mum's big cuddle,
My dad's tickling ways,
My brother's laughs,
My best friend's tickles,
My gran's biscuits.

Best forgotten

My cat's illnesses,
My dog's problems,
My mum's shouting at me,
My dad's golf trips,
My brother's horrible feelings,
My best friend's nastiness,
My gran's boring tea.

Mollie Rowland (9)
Chapel-en-le-Frith Primary School

The Lion

He lies in the outback,
Eating zebras and meat,
Sneaking in the bushes.
The strongest animal in the land;
The scariest animal in the land.
Just when people come for a picnic,
He will bite off their hands.

Aaron Sharp (9)
Chapel-en-le-Frith Primary School

My Apostrophe Poem

Best remembered

My sister's PS2,
My cousin's Xbox,
My mum's car,
My dad's knowledge,
My gran's house,
My friend's generosity,
My uncle's DVD player.

Best forgotten

My sister's selfishness,
My cousin's nagging,
My mum's threatening,
My dad's shouting,
My gran's forces,
My uncle's children.

Mark Watson (9)
Chapel-en-le-Frith Primary School

The Komodo Dragon

His grasping claws pull his prey towards him.
He takes one snap, like lightning, into his dark, dark mouth.
His cracking tail smashes the rock, like a crane breaking rock.
He is as still as a statue in a cave.
His next meal passes by and he jolts forward, *crack!*

Timothy Greenhalgh (9)
Chapel-en-le-Frith Primary School

My Apostrophe Poem

Best remembered

My guinea pig's yellow bottom,
My rabbit's long ears,
My dog's soft fur,
My bird's warm feathers,
My mum's lovely ways,
My dad's blue house,
My brother's red cheeks.

Worst remembered

My mum's smelly car,
My horse's strong feet,
My brother's big mole,
My mum's handwriting,
My dog's licks,
My friend's eyes.

Hannah Mycock (8)
Chapel-en-le-Frith Primary School

The Cougar

He waits for his prey like a poacher,
In the dense snow, he crouches.
He approaches his prey in total stealth.
All the time he watches his target.
He moves to the back with his prey.
He pounces like an arrow from a bow.

Matthew Green (9)
Chapel-en-le-Frith Primary School

The Crocodile

He glides so stealthily.
He looks like a log on the water.
He swims so near to the bank.
The water is so still.
Then suddenly he sees his prey.
He shoots forward like a thunderbolt
And grabs the zebra's head.

David Twaites (8)
Chapel-en-le-Frith Primary School

Winter

I like the snow
I go sledging
I don't like the snow
I get wet
I like the snow
I build a snowman
I don't like the snow
I don't like people chucking snowballs
I like the snow
I make snow angels
I don't like the snow
I hate tripping up.

Sam Hesketh
Chapel-en-le-Frith Primary School

The Dolphin

Oh how you swim,
Your skin so soft and shimmering.
We all stare at you as your fin
Cuts through the water so elegantly.
You can always choose the right spot for us.
So soft, so soft.

Bethanie Williamson (9)
Chapel-en-le-Frith Primary School

The Dark Secret

The middle of the woods has a secret, a deep, dark secret.
In a cave the secret lurks, waiting, waiting.
There it is, consuming the light and spreading the dark.
The shadows are its domain, waiting to pounce on unsuspecting prey.
To feed off their fears and destroy their happiness
And that is the dark secret that no one knows.

Jack Shepperd (11)
Denby Free CE (Aided) Primary School

Christmas

'Twas the night before Christmas where all Christmas spirits fly,
All because of Santa that falls right down from the sky.
Santa says the best things are the mince pies.
Believe in Santa, he never tells lies.
Oh yes, there's still the behaviour list.
You have to be good, Santa insists.

Hannah Glenn (9)
Denby Free CE (Aided) Primary School

Arachnid

There's an arachnid in the room
I'll tell you what it's like,
Its head is like a golf ball,
Its body is like a tennis ball,
Its legs are like pitchforks,
Its fangs are like daggers,

'Come quickly Mum!
Aaarrrggghhh!'

Matthew Manley (9)
Denby Free CE (Aided) Primary School

A Potter's Life (1830's)

A potter's life is tough,
Managing to produce enough,
Living on a tight wage
Being treated like a slave.

Throwing clay on the wheel,
With only the ground for us to kneel,
Finishing up with a beer bottle,
All of us working at full throttle.

A potter's life is tough,
Managing to produce enough,
Living on a tight wage,
Being treated like a slave.

Delivering our products straight to the checking room,
Waiting and waiting till the checker looms,
Finding out the pots are fine is what we want to hear,
Finding out the pots are wrong is our worst fear.

A potter's life is tough,
Managing to produce enough.
Living on a tight wage,
Being treated like a slave.

Charlotte Richardson (10)
Denby Free CE (Aided) Primary School

At Home

At home my bedroom is
big and cosy

At home my mum and dad
are kind and loving

At home my pet rabbit
is soft, warm and playful

At home the meal I love
is chilli con carne.

Alex Taylor (10)
Denby Free CE (Aided) Primary School

Denby Pottery

Oh Denby Pottery
How different you are
From then to now, you're different by far.

Clay, clay
You do not change
But we can make and play.

Oh Denby Pottery
How different you are
From then to now, you're different by far.

Clay, clay
You are so old
You don't know how many pots we've sold.

Oh Denby Pottery
How different you are
From then to now, you're different by far.

Clay, clay
You are a success
But you sure make a lot of mess!

Oh Denby Pottery
How different you are
From then to now, you're different by far.

Clay, clay
You've been in lots of hands
Even in my grandad's nan's.

Oh Denby Pottery
How different you are
From then to now, you're different by far.

Clay, clay
We're proud of you
So carry on what you must do.

Chloe Barlow (9)
Denby Free CE (Aided) Primary School

At Home

At home
My bedroom is small and cosy and warm
and it welcomes me when I come in.

At home
My parents are nice and loving,
My mum is beautiful and my dad is cool
but my sisters, except for baby Holly are silly.

At home my games are the best that I like,
My PS2 is amazing and you could play
almost anything on it.

At home
It's the best thing in my life because it's
Wicked and I love my home with my parents.
my sisters and my baby sister

Daniel Middleton (10)
Denby Free CE (Aided) Primary School

The Woods

As I walk along the narrow path
No animals in sight
All in hibernation, warm and snug.
Trees everywhere, flowing in the wind,
As the snow falls down on my soft hat and the stony steps.
I trample along through the white woods,
Across the menacing sky, see the tree shapes glow
Watch the snow blow.
As I run to the end, I jump over the stile
And put on a great big smile
Now I'm out of the spooky woods.

Jody Crooks (11)
Denby Free CE (Aided) Primary School

My Family

My brother is a wild animal,
roaming the jungle.

My mum is as mad as a bull,
when it sees red.

My dad is as calm as a fox,
hunting in the night.

My mum's partner is as loud as a chimpanzee,
mad, screaming in the jungle tops.

My cats are as wild as a tiger,
when prey is spotted.

My mum's partner's children are as crazy as chimps,
swinging around the jungle.

My nana and grandad are as nice as can be,
helping me.

Daniel Sarson (11)
Denby Free CE (Aided) Primary School

The Writer Of This Poem
(Based on 'The Writer of This Poem' by Roger McGough)

The writer of this poem
Is taller than a lamp post,
As keen as an Olympic gold medallist,
As beautiful as a queen.

As smooth as velvet
As quick as lightning,
As clean as the dentists,
As clever as a tick
As quiet as a mouse.

This writer is the best!

Emily Allsop (10)
Denby Free CE (Aided) Primary School

At Home

At home my bedroom is quiet, cosy, warm
and welcomes me when I walk in.

At home my dad is caring, loving, loyal,
kind, funny and a fun person to play with.

At home, my cat is thin and a bit poorly.

At home my favourite game is darts
and I play darts with my dad.

At home the meal I love the most is
pasta with melted cheese on top.

At home my best friend is funny,
caring, loyal and fun to play with.

Shannon Jarvis (9)
Denby Free CE (Aided) Primary School

The Writer Of This Poem

(Based on 'The Writer Of This Poem' by Roger McGough)

Is smaller than a mouse
As bold as a monkey
As fast as a cheetah

As bright as a light
As thin as a pencil
As brave as a knight
As potty as an athlete

And overall, the writer of
This poem is very, very musical.

Lucy Mellor (9)
Denby Free CE (Aided) Primary School

Denby Pottery

Oh I work here day by day,
Watching the fire burn away.
Oh I work here night by night,
Working here by candlelight.

Denby Pottery being as it is
There's plenty of work for Mr Bourne
Well, it is 'is!

Oh I work here day by day,
Watching the fire burn away.
Oh I work here night by night,
Working here by candlelight.

A bloke broke a couple of pots today
So then that'll be more recycled clay
Unlucky for 'im
That'll be three shillings off 'is pay!

Oh I work here day by day,
Watching the fire burn away.
Oh I work here night by night,
Working here by candlelight.

I dropped a few pots this mornin'
Turned round just as they were fallin'.
So now what can I say?
That'll be three shillings off me pay!

Oh I work here day by day,
Watching the fire burn away.
Oh I work here night by night,
Working here by candlelight.

Madeleine Walker (10)
Denby Free CE (Aided) Primary School

The Start Of The Pottery

In 1809 William ran it
Then it was Joseph
Not everything would fit
Dust was the sniff.

'Best ever clay,' said William Bourne.
The miners were digging away.

Handmake the pots
And try and make enough
Put them on the dotties
A potter's life was tough.

'Best ever clay,' said William Bourne.
The miners were digging away.

They work by candlelight
And put clay in saggars
Not a good sight
To have a potter's life.

'Best ever clay,' said William Bourne.
The miners were digging away.

Make 1,440 half-pint jugs
You'll get three shillings.
The miners dug
So the potters get paid.

'Best ever clay,' said William Bourne.
The miners were digging away.

Jack Lawrence (11)
Denby Free CE (Aided) Primary School

Fantasy Life

Pirates are cruel,
And they're cool.

        Fairies are bright
        And they shine in the night.

Goblins are rude
And vile and crude.

        Trolls are mean
        And never clean.

Pixies are evil
And do things that are illegal.

        Witches are bad
        And make people sad.

Dragons are strong,
And do things wrong.

        What a fantasy life!

Bronwyn Stevens (10)
Granby Junior School

Ice Creams

Soft and creamy
Gentle and dreamy (chocolate)
What do I mean?
Ice cream, ice cream!

Have it with jelly
It's best in my belly.
Vanilla, banana, chocolate,
Any kind - I just can't wait.

Jemma Browning (8)
Granby Junior School

My Pet Huggles

My pet Huggles
  Is just like me
    Swirling in the bed
      Warm as could be

My pet Huggles
  Happy as could be
    Eating carrots and
      Lettuce just as they do

My pet Huggles
  Knowing what to do
    Doing the same thing
      Copying just as I do.

My pet Huggles
  Has a little love
    In the bed he goes
      Upstairs and downstairs.

All the way he goes
  Flapping his ears with his little pink nose
    Bless the poor rabbit, give him a show or two.

Paige Bailey (8)
Granby Junior School

Safety First

Make sure to tell where you're going
There's no way of knowing
If someone is ready
To kidnap you, so stay steady
So that you're here
So your mum can call you 'dear'.

Kyle Scott (10)
Granby Junior School

My Friends

Chloe is as fast as a lion,
Chloe is as funny as a clown.
Chloe is as caring as an owl,
That's my friend Chloe!

Michael sticks his arm out like a bird,
Michael is as funny as a chipmunk,
Michael is fast at timestables, like a cheetah.
That's my friend Michael!

Hannah is as small as an ant
Hannah sings like a bird in the sky,
Hannah plays like a swan in the pond.
That's my friend Hannah!

Sam is as kind as a monkey,
Sam is as silly as a clown.
Sam is as serious as an owl,
That's my friend Sam!

They're my best friends, Chloe, Michael, Hannah and Sam,
They're my best friends in school.

Sophie Barratt (8)
Granby Junior School

The Big Fat Frog

The big fat frog
Sitting on the log.
He makes a lot of noise
I wonder if he can play with toys!
The big fat frog jumps around,
He sat on the lily pad
And then he went a little mad!

Anya Holland (8)
Granby Junior School

Day And Night

In the day the city is noisy
All the people are rushing around.
Cars are rushing down the street,
Horns are beeping, beep! Beep! Beep! Beep!

Cats are climbing trees and chasing birds,
Dogs are going for walks and chasing balls.
Mums and dads are going shopping
In the night, the city is silent
All the people are asleep.

There are no cars rushing around,
There are no cats climbing trees.
There are no dogs chasing balls,
All the shops are closed.

But in the morning, the city will
Be noisy again!

Emily Tindall (8)
Granby Junior School

My Imaginary World

My imaginary world is very, very pretty,
Some people call it precious world Kitty.
My imaginary world is like my family,
People say my world is like me.
I call my world - hmm! Let's see!
I call my world - just like me.
My world has got lots of people in it,
Dolphins swimming in and out,
It is very pretty, I admit.

Louise Priest (9)
Granby Junior School

A Dolphin

The dolphin swims in the sea all day
He goes down to the bottom all the way
he J
    U
     M
      P
       S up high, right to the sky
with his friends following him.

When he swims his tail goes
W   O   S
 H   O   H
through the cool blue sea.

'Wow!' shout the people, 'that's so cool!'

Cally Smith (8)
Granby Junior School

My Dog Jake

Fluffy and brown is my dog Jake,
He eats a lot but is as thin as a rake.
He wags his tail and runs around and
When he barks, he makes a loud sound
When I take him for a walk -
Sometimes I wish that he could talk
Then he could tell me what he would like to do
And when he needed to go for a poo!
I wouldn't change him at all,
If I need him, I only call.

Amber Shanahan (10)
Granby Junior School

Meet My Five Best Friends

Meet lovely Holly
She's got a big dolly.

                    Meet Miss Amy
                    She needs to pay me!

Meet Lauren
She's foreign.

                    Meet Lucy G
                    She likes to play with me.

Meet Lucy C
She plays bulldog with me.

Natalie Brown (10)
Granby Junior School

Saying Goodbye!

Saying goodbye
Made lots of people cry
On that cold January day.

I will never forget
The way I felt
Looking at sad faces
And lots of people filling those empty spaces.

The music played
And some words were said
About what a special person she was.

I said goodbye to my aunt
Forget her! - I can't!

Demi Drew (9)
Granby Junior School

The Hundred Percent Weird Horror House

When you walk through the hundred percent horror house
You might see a frightened little mouse.
You might think that you're alone
But you're not, you're surrounded by a lot of bone.
As you close your bloodshot eyes
The hopeless spirits start to rise.
When they brush past your soft, white skin
That's when the terror starts to begin.
After the birds have settled in their nest
The ghosts start to do what they do best.
One has a tie, one has a bow and one has a beard
Anyway, like I said, it's a horror house
That is very, very weird.

Kirby Edwards (8)
Granby Junior School

My Fantasy Life

Pirates are mean
Pirates are cruel
Pirates are naughty
And so not cool

Witches cast spells
On human beings
Witches are messy
And do not clean

Fairies are sneaky
And come out at night
Fairies are little
And shine in the light.

Lucy Graham (10)
Granby Junior School

Pyjamas

I'm a pair of silk pyjamas
I'm as comfy as can be
I keep people snug and warm
Until the following day
They take me off
Throw me down
That's the end of the day
They put me on the very next night
Then that's the end of that.

Charlotte Heseltine (9)
Granby Junior School

There Was An Old Woman From Cadbury Land

There was an old woman from Cadbury Land
Who played day and night in the chocolate sand
When she got bored, she went back home to Chocolate Lane
And ate a piece of chocolate straight from the windowpane
When she had finished, she watched her son
Play in the chocolate band.

Chloe Wood (11)
Granby Junior School

You Are A Star

You are a star and you didn't know it,
You are a star and you really show it.
You might not realise it but I do -
I want to be a star like you.

Olivia Gibson (10)
Granby Junior School

Hospitals

Hospitals are very sad places,
Because you see very sad faces.
If you bang your head
You may be put in a bed.
Ambulances dash about
And never give a shout.
You may see people with bashes
Or even people with rashes!

Matthew Ashley (11)
Granby Junior School

Miss April Dawn

April is a beauty
She has got bright blonde hair
And little baby curls
She has got adorable blue eyes
And a little pink nose
And she wears a little pink top
And little purple joggers
And that's our little
April Dawn!

Francessca Wilcock (9)
Granby Junior School

Seasons

Summer has its sunny sun
Spring is fun and bouncy,
Autumn is a lot of windy fun,
And winter is cold and icy.
So many seasons, so much fun
It would top it off if I could share
It with someone.

Emily Buck (10)
Granby Junior School

We Care For You!

Now we are here
We can share our secrets,
And do things together
And to learn to care for people we know.
With dreams about friends and family,
And happy thoughts for life
And when we have a bad turn.
Have a think
And maybe you'll change the next day.

Carly Baker (9)
Granby Junior School

My Rabbit

My rabbit is called Hoppy
And smells like a poppy.

He is black and white,
And comes alive at night.

We had a race
But he has a pretty face.

He hops all over the house,
Like a little mouse.

Chloe Rachel Foulkes (8)
Granby Junior School

The Waterfall

Jumping, leaping, crashing
Flying over the cliff edge.
It hits the rocks and splashes
Up foam and froth and mist.
Then it calms, makes its
Way to its next cliff.

Nikita Stevenson (8)
Granby Junior School

Grandparents

Grandma's in the kitchen
Baking bread for dinner
Grandad's reading the paper
Trying to pick a winner!
Both of them are special
So that's why I'm telling you.
I want to be just like them
When I'm a grandma too!

Holly Bramley (10)
Granby Junior School

The Stars

The stars are so bright in the night,
when it is morning, you can't see them but
when it is night you can see them!
Because they are so bright!
When you go out at night look out for
Lovely bright, twinkling stars!

Jackie Spencer (8)
Granby Junior School

My Family

My family is so special to me,
So I like to see them and invite them to tea.
When I don't see my family for a while
I start to lose my sense and style.
I love my family, whatever they do
And I hope they love me too!

Abigail Sisson (9)
Granby Junior School

The Wicked Spell

Hocus pocus, bubble and pop,
Eye of giant, bogie, snot.
Ant's body, man's flesh,
Witch's cackle
Watch it bubble!

Hocus pocus, bubble and pop,
Fur of cat, ear of dog.
Lion's tail, a pint of spit,
Then watch it, watch it
Go pop, bang, whizz and crunch!

Amy Brooks (9)
Granby Junior School

Firework Fly

Fireworks, fireworks, flying in the sky
Blue ones, red ones, flying so high.
They *crackle! Bang and boom!*
Through the night sky, each one
Zooms!

Laurie Plant (8)
Granby Junior School

The Butterfly

I am a butterfly
I am as light as a feather
Then I approach my wings into the sky
And off I go, flying with the birds
And what a beautiful sight it is.

Amy Lockwood (9)
Granby Junior School

Leaves

Suntanned leaves flowing in the air
Excited leaves jumping everywhere
Orange
Browns
Yellows too
Many colours of every hue!

Crispy leaves, crunching underfoot
Burn your fire till it all turns to soot.
Orange
Browns
Yellows too
Many colours of every hue!

The huge tall trees, standing up proud
All the family sitting in a crowd.
Orange
Browns
Yellows too
Many colours of every hue!

Rebecca Baraona (10)
Grindleford Primary School

On The Lawn In The Morning

A pair of sticks
A hat that is dusty
A carrot
(A clean, orange one).

A scarf (that is knitted)
A pile of stones
(As dry as bones).

Who was here?
A snowman.

Ruth Jackson (8)
Grindleford Primary School

In Bed

Last night,
When I was in bed,
Snow spread
Across the fields.
The garden vanished
Underneath a furry blanket!
The cold snow blew its white breath,
The next morning when I woke up
A world covered in white
Overnight!

David Gill (9)
Grindleford Primary School

Footprints

In the garden
I saw my footprints
And other footprints too.
My dad went down to the shed
Next-door's cat crossed the lawn
My sister fell over
I'm a snow detective!

George Wrench (8)
Grindleford Primary School

Footprints

Across the white covered park,
Hedgehogs' footprints are all around, in the dark.
When all the children are asleep,
The snow comes down in a great big heap,
Then the morning comes and the sun is here.
Let's play more, next year.

Joanne Barber (9)
Grindleford Primary School

Kennings

My dog
A leg cuddler
A mouth dribbler
An excited howler
A nifty runner
A furry blob

My hamster
A pouch filler
A cage climber
A finger biter
A night watcher
A fluffy ball.

Jack Maynard (9)
Grindleford Primary School

Kennings Wolf

A night howler
A caring mother
A vicious growler
A deadly biter
A pack hunter.

Harry William Bushell (11)
Grindleford Primary School

My Rabbit

A hand licker
A quick runner
A lettuce cruncher
A great listener
A silent sleeper.

William Gratton (9)
Grindleford Primary School

Fly And Shark

Fly:
Sneaky fly
Searching for food
Get off my dinner
Swat!

Shark:
Death bringer
Bone cruncher
Jaw dropper
Toe shredder
Leg taker
Fish watcher.

Freddie Thomas Reynolds (10)
Grindleford Primary School

My Old Cat

An elegant walker,
A purring pouncer.
A night hunter,
A day dreamer.
A warm cushion.

Holly Ragdale (11)
Grindleford Primary School

Baboon

Cheeky grinner
Bum flasher
Troop leader
War machine
Cliff tracer

Sam Willis (11)
Grindleford Primary School

Kennings

A view of a panda:
A black and white furball
An eye-patched eater
A lazy lump
A bamboo chewer
A plodding mover

A view of a sloth:
A hanging sleeper
A berry eater
A slow mover
A leaf hoover
A bending backbone.

Rebecca Bowman (11)
Grindleford Primary School

Kennings Alligator

A meat shredder
A swamp lurker
A slow walker
A fierce fighter
An egg layer.

Robbie Jackson (9)
Grindleford Primary School

Turtle

Lettuce eater
Slow plodder
Moving house
Sleepy dozer
Friendly creature.

Beth Willis (9)
Grindleford Primary School

Kennings

Pig:
A food eater
A chubby ball
A pink rooter
A round sniffer
A dirty oinker.

Dog:
A fast runner
A food hogger
A door scratcher
A bone cruncher
A loving parent.

Charlie Bushell (9)
Grindleford Primary School

Kennings Penguin

A fish cruncher
An ice slipper
A slow waddler
A proud white breast
An intelligent hugger.

Meryn Norman (9)
Grindleford Primary School

Kennings Fighting Fish

A swift swimmer
A deadly fighter
A colourful glimmer
A nasty biter
A territory keeper.

Liam Friend (10)
Grindleford Primary School

Kennings

Hyena:
A pouncing predator,
A super stalker,
A quick walker,
A mincing menace,
A laughing lounger.

My hamster:
A pouch packer,
A wheel whizzer,
A super stalker,
A brocolli bruncher,
A carrot cruncher,
Fast footed,
Big gutted,
A hole digger.

Craig Wilson (11)
Grindleford Primary School

Kennings Lion

A sleek stalker
A team worker
A silent ambusher
A throat biter
A selfish eater.

Josh Cadman (10)
Grindleford Primary School

Links Adventure

There once was a boy called Link
With a sword and shield
He was on a huge adventure
But he made sure his weapons were sealed.

He then started his adventure
Defeating enemies and bosses
But in some places
The enemies hid in vases.

Then he came to the final boss
Who had the triforce in his hand
His name was Ganondorf
He put evilness upon Hyrule land.

Link had to use his weapons
To defeat him
Link took a little damage
But surely he was going to win.

Then he defeated Ganondorf
That was the end of him
Then a blue flash shone around Link
And when it was carrying him away
The sky went dim.

He then found himself in the Sage Room
Where the six Sages lay
The Sages formed the triforce triangle
Then peace returned to Hyrule the Sages way.

Ali Chaudhry (9)
Hardwick Junior School

Weather

Spring, summer, autumn and winter
All of them are different.

Spring is the time to clean
And to plant your seeds
Out pop animals from
Their homes
We are happy again
To see sunshine.

Summer has come now
And it's hot, hot, hot!
Flowers have grown and now
Grass is greener than ever.
What will be next?
However do we know?

Autumn is here, it is getting cold
No more sunshine, all has gone
Flowers now have died, leaves are falling off
As I walk, all is crunch, crunch and crunch!

Winter's approached now, it's colder than ever
Falling snow, all the pavements glittering white.
Be careful not to slip
That would not be fun!

Selina Hussain (10)
Hardwick Junior School

Pit A Pot

Who will pit-a-pot?
I'm hotter than a hot,
I have no daughter
To pour on cool water.
Oh who will help who?
Is it you? Is it you?

Maimuna Saliha (10)
Hardwick Junior School

The Jungle

I was walking through the jungle
With a Coke can in my hand
Singing, 'Ha! Everybody!
I'm the queen of the land.'
But suddenly I looked up a tree
Only to see a monkey trying
To throw bananas at me!
So I fizzed my Coke up to 90°C
And shot the monkey
Sitting up in the tree.

I was walking through the jungle
With nothing in my hand
Singing, 'Ha! Everybody
I'm the queen of the land.'
But suddenly I looked near a tree
And there was my mum, calling to me
So I charged my leg up to 9°C
And ran to my mum
Getting stung by bees.

Stacy Ann Shepherd (10)
Hardwick Junior School

Falling Snow

Falling snow, cold, freezing cold,
Snow, fast, falling down,
Snow, soft and crunching on the ground
Ice slipping people, very fast.

Snow is very white and bright
Soft as a cuddly toy
And as smooth as my kitchen floor
Snowflakes falling nice and slow.

Marcus Ward (10)
Hardwick Junior School

Ancient Castle And The Weird King

Once there was a king,
Who always sings
Who once had a butler
But he was a very dangerous butler
Because he carried a cuttler.
One night, there was a storm
And the king sat on a pin and
Bumped his chin.
The king was in a bad mood,
So he ordered some food
But this food wasn't any ordinary food
It was talking food.
The king was so happy
That he went to his room
But he kept the whole castle awake.

Jade Jessica Weeks (10)
Hardwick Junior School

Christmas On Mars

There once was a bunch of aliens,
Who were celebrating Christmas on Mars,
Dancing round a Christmas crater
Eating from little glass jars.

It was snowy on their winter wonderland,
The space slugs were doing the slime dance,
Serving cakes, maggots and rock sticks to sell,
Everyone else was in a trance.

All the family gathered round for tea,
Lots of laughs and stories to tell,
It was lovely to see my long lost love,
The only thing was, she cast a spell.

Oliver Jacob Culley de Lange (9)
Hardwick Junior School

The Green Man

There once was a green man
Who had a magic fan that spun a hundred miles per hour,
He has climbed the highest tower,
Whilst he was up there, he ate Skittles which were sour.
He is as green and as ugly as a frog,
His hair is spiked, like a hedgehog,
He wants to talk, like a cool boy,
But he speaks like a robotic toy.

Zoheb Hussain (10)
Hardwick Junior School

The Alien

I know this alien, this alien named Woo,
This alien was born in an alien zoo.
This alien was made of alien goo.

This alien was kind
He had a good mind,
Didn't even commit a crime!

I know this alien, this alien named Woo,
He was small and kind and friendly too!

Mandeep Singh Sangha (9)
Hardwick Junior School

Time

Moody Monday, still half asleep,
Terrible Tuesday, scary secrets to keep.
Wet Wednesday, can't go out to play,
Thankful Thursday, sunny all day.
Finally Friday, end of the week,
Sunny Saturday, friends with whom to speak.
Sorry Sunday, of all the cheek!
Another day and another week.

Poppy Sephton Clark (9)
Hardwick Junior School

Fireworks

Fireworks, fireworks,
bright and beautiful.
Fireworks, fireworks,
burst out like shooting stars
Fireworks, fireworks,
fun to watch.
Fireworks, fireworks,
don't go too near.
Fireworks, fireworks,
shoot up like a rocket.
Fireworks, fireworks,
ask an adult to light
Fireworks, fireworks,
colourful as a rainbow
Fireworks, fireworks,
noisy to my ears,
Fireworks, fireworks,
shining like a star.

Mubasher Sajid (10)
Hardwick Junior School

The Ocean

Fishes jumping out from the ocean,
Splish, splosh, splish, splosh!
Dolphins jumping up and down,
Deep beneath the ocean, sharks lurk for their prey
Now the sun is going down,
Every animal stops until another day.

Now the sun is coming up,
Everybody plays again,
The fish are jumping.
The dolphins are jumping up and down,
Sharks are looking for prey once again.

Adam Brown (9)
Hardwick Junior School

Winter's Day

Snow falls onto the trees,
Snow falls onto the ground,
Snow falls onto the houses.

Footprints of animals in the snow,
Snowballs, snowmen,
Crystal drops hanging off trees,
Sparkling diamonds hang off the windows,
Magical dust of snow,
Birds singing in the treetops and looking for food,
Ponds of ice,
Frost on the wood,
Mystical skies,
Daffodil bulbs pushing through the white ground.

Shelly Wilkinson
Hartsthorne CE Primary School

Amy's Pony

Amy's pony was very bony,
She fed it some corn
Just after it was born.
He shot up like a rocket
And went in everyone's pocket,
Looking for food to put him in the mood
For dancing and prancing.
When he was able to go in the stable
She named him of course,
But he was such a cheeky horse
She called him Monkey!

Amy Jenkinson (9)
Hartsthorne CE Primary School

No One Knows

Is that a monster in the frozen pond
Or just an old football been there since summer?

No one knows, no one knows

Are they delicious ice creams
On extra long sticks
Or just teasels covered in snow?

No one knows, no one knows

Is that a load of giant spiders
Hiding in the snow
Or just some plants covered up?

No one knows, no one knows

And has someone covered the snow in glitter
Or was it always like that?

No one knows, no one knows
Nobody knows.

Rebecca Redfern (10)
Hartshorne CE Primary School

A Winter Wonderland

The snow was glistening in the sun,
Birds were singing in the trees,
Icicles dangling from the shimmering houses,
A person was walking down the road,
It was as quiet, as quiet,
She could not hear anything,
Suddenly she looked and saw,
Children dancing and playing,
In a wonderful land.

Romany Freeman (9)
Hartshorne CE Primary School

Untitled

Footprints in the snow
Ho, ho, ho, ho
The snow starts to glisten
And the animals stop and listen

The icicles crack and fall
The old crow starts to call
We're in the snow dust
And all the roads have an icy crust

It's a white winter wonderland
And everywhere is covered in sand
My garden's covered in snow
There are shimmering crystals everywhere I go

There are footprints in the snow
Ho, ho, ho, ho, ho.

William Alexander (11)
Hartshorne CE Primary School

Winter Wonderland

I woke up to see what morning would bring
I looked through the window to hear the birds sing.
All I saw was white sand,
I found my garden was a winter wonderland.
I went outside in gloves and hat,
In wonderland I sat.
A shiver down my spine,
At last, I knew, the day was mine.

George Fletcher (10)
Hartshorne CE Primary School

Winter Land

I open a door to a winter scene
A blizzard of snow I'm very keen
I made a snowman, the very best
Not to mention it had a vest
The winter breeze makes me cold
I feel like making a snowman mould
I'm sad that I have to go
A winter land covered in snow.

Alex Patrick (9)
Hartshorne CE Primary School

The Writer Of This Poem
(Based on 'The Writer Of This Poem' by Roger McGough)

The writer of this poem,
Is as sweet as a baby,
As funny as a clown,
As lovely as a lady.

As slithery as a snake,
As funny as Mr T,
As little as a lake,
As cool as that boy Lee.

As jolly as a mum,
As peaceful as can be,
As juicy as a plum,
As hot as a cup of tea.

The writer of this poem,
Is as massive as a house,
As happy as a fruit,
(Or so the poem says.)

Catherine Timbrell (10)
Measham CE Primary School

The Writer Of This Poem
(Based on 'The Writer Of This Poem' by Roger McGough)

The writer of this poem
Is a little funny
As funny as Mr T
As little as a bee.

As sweet as a sheet
As jolly as a prickly piece of holly
As playful and as peaceful, as graceful as can be
As juicy as a raspberry just like me.

As tender as sender
As bleak as mid-winter
As blonde as a pond
As happy as me.

The writer of this poem
Is quiet as a mouse
Of course it's me.

Lucy Lakin (11)
Measham CE Primary School

Well Done!

Well done, your work is great.
Well done, you've got it right.
Well done, it's wonderful.
Well done, you've done the test.
Well done, you're in the golden book.
Well done, you've got the job!

Adora Mottram (7)
Measham CE Primary School

Kennings

Hay nibbler
Celery muncher
Bridge climber
Nose twitcher
Grass eater
Water gulper

To make a guinea pig

Wave jumper
Fish eater
Deep sea diver
Shark scarer
Voice speaker

To make a dolphin.

Jordan Haynes (11)
Measham CE Primary School

My Life

My life is fun, like a big iced bun.
My life is funny, like a springtime bunny.
My life has power, like a summer flower.
My life is bright, like stars at night.
My life is the fire that I admire.
My life is a pillow, soft like a pussy willow.
My life plays all day.
My life's the best.
I like my life every day!

Georgia Banton (9)
Measham CE Primary School

The Writer Of This Poem
(Based on 'The Writer Of This Poem' by Roger McGough)

The writer of this poem,
Is as wavy as the sea,
As soft as a kitten,
As sweet as can be.

As tough as old boots,
As elegant as a ballet dancer,
As bouncy as a kangaroo,
As colourful as a rainbow.

As fresh as a daisy,
As big as Saturn,
As fast as lightning,
As bright as a lantern.

The writer of this poem,
Strikes people in a daze,
She's as clever as a calculator,
(Or so the poem says!)

Anna Aldersley (10)
Measham CE Primary School

The Ghost

Ghost and ghouls come out to play
Frightening all the kids away
Ghost and ghouls all in white
Ooh what an ugly sight
Ghost and ghouls dance and sing
Like a fairy on her wing
Ghost and ghouls go away
Of a break of a new day.

Christopher Fisher (11)
Measham CE Primary School

My Alphabet Poem

A was for an anchor.
B bought it.
C caught it.
D dropped it.
E had eaten it.
F fought it.
G gulped.
H hooked it.
I injured it.
J juggled it.
K kicked it.
L longed for it.
M mummified it.
N nicked it.
O opened it.
P pulled it.
Q quacked with it.
R rattled it.
S stepped on it.
T tricked it.
U understood it.
V voted for it.
XYZ and ampersand all wished for one to help
Them land.

Lauren Mason (10)
Measham CE Primary School

Cinquain

Ferret
Eating my food
Jumping around the cage
I like to hide in the paper
It's great.

Kyle Sanders (11)
Measham CE Primary School

The Writer Of This Poem
(Based on 'The Writer Of This Poem' by Roger McGough)

The writer of this poem is
As fast as a speeding bullet,
As tall as the Empire State Building
And as brainy as can be.

As small as a mouse,
As tough as a house
And as powerful as a warhead.

As clumsy as Jar Jar Binx,
As gentle as a dolphin
And as interesting as a horror movie.

The writer of this poem
Never seizes to amaze,
He's one in a million
Or so the poem says.

Josh Grascia (10)
Measham CE Primary School

My Funky Friends!

My funny friends are
As beautiful as butterflies,
That fly around all day,
As kind as Winnie the Pooh,
Sharing out his honey,
My best mates are
As kind as Florence Nightingale,
As clever as a tick,
As cuddly as a panda.

Emma Roach (11)
Measham CE Primary School

The Writer Of This Poem
(Based on 'The Writer Of This Poem' by Roger McGough)

The writer of this poem,
Is as smart as Einstein,
As fit as a fiddle,
As twisty as a vine.

As bright as day,
As wobbly as jelly,
As darling as a daffodil,
As funny as the telly.

As fast as a cheetah,
As quiet as a mouse,
As tall as a tree,
As safe as a house.

The writer of this poem,
Has nothing to do but gaze,
Up at the stars at night
(Or so the poem says!)

Ashleigh McClane-Smith (10)
Measham CE Primary School

Kennings A Road

Lorry lover,
Child killer,
Paint wearer,
Bike bearer,
Car carrier,
People barrier,
Hedgehog squasher,
Nature husher,
Animal musher,
Traffic rusher.

Victoria Ince (11)
Measham CE Primary School

My Whizzo Warplane

My whizzo warplane is as fast as a rocket
soaring into space.
My whizzo warplane is as scary as a dragon
zooming in the sky.
My whizzo warplane is more powerful
than a Lancaster bomber.
My whizzo warplane is stronger than
reinforced diamond.
My whizzo warplane can fly high
above the clouds.
My whizzo warplane has machine guns
more powerful than a rocket launcher.
My whizzo warplane is more dynamic
than a racing car.
My whizzo warplane is camouflaged
in the night sky.
My whizzo warplane is all in my head now
I've woken up and got out of bed.

Ben Thompson (10)
Measham CE Primary School

My Bouncy Bunny

My bouncy bunny is
As tall as a skyscraper that touches the sky
As pretty as a picture hanging on the wall
As bouncy as a trampoline
As fast as a cheetah running over a plain
As cuddly as a teddy bear, I give him a hug
As a feather on a warm bed
As funny as a clown juggling

My bouncy bunny is the best in the world!

Bethany Coleman (11)
Measham CE Primary School

The Writer Of This Poem . . .
(Based on 'The Writer Of This Poem' by Roger McGough)

The writer of this poem
Is cooler than the Arctic
As funny as Mr T
As pretty as can be.

As fit as a fiddle
As hard as a rock
As clean as a white sheet
As square as a block.

As scared as a mouse
As stunning as Britney
As fresh as a mint
As tall as a house.

The writer of this poem
Is always in a daze
She's the best ever
(Or so the poem says!)

Yasmin Tills (10)
Measham CE Primary School

My Fast Falcon

My fast falcon is . . .
As quick as thunder, striking the city at night,
As marvellous as a magician, performing tricks in the light,
As scary as the leaves, rustling in the wind,
As silly as a toy clown, that had just been binned,
As colourful as a rainbow, shining in the sun,
As funny as men in black, playing with a toy gun,
As spoilt as a little brat, playing with her toys,
Playing games with other birds and making lots of noise!
Just trust my falcon!

Michaela Smeaton (10)
Measham CE Primary School

The Writer Of This Poem
(Based on 'The Writer Of This Poem' by Roger McGough)

The writer of this poem
Is sweeter than a lolly,
As safe as a padlock,
As sharp as holly.

As pretty as flower,
As clumsy as jelly,
As light as a feather,
As warm as a welly.

As tall as a giraffe,
As peaceful as a kite,
As funny as a clown,
As soothing as the night.

The writer of this poem is
As gripping as plays,
As clever as a calculator
(Or so the poem says!)

Loretta Hull (10)
Measham CE Primary School

Kennings

A wave crasher
A boat smasher

A fish killer
A soaking pillar

A shark finder
A storm binder.

Parris Wileman (11)
Measham CE Primary School

My Amazing Guinea Pig

My amazing guinea pig,
Is as fast as lightning
Falling through the trees.
As cute as a kitten,
Sleeping in its basket.
As greedy as a pig,
At dinner time.
As loud as an
Elephant too
Excited to play
As smooth as a
Bed cover laid for the night.
As tender as a chicken.
As scared as a mouse.
As jumpy as a kangaroo
My amazing guinea pig
Is the best ever!

Grace Noble (10)
Measham CE Primary School

Swap? Sell? Small Adds Sell Fast

1968 Mum. Good sleeper at night
Needs a few repairs on the light.
She's got two seats and she always leaks.
She's always tired when she's fired;
We fill her up with a large cup.
She's never sick but she goes tick.
I'm not selling her never ever!

1965 Dad. Runs out all the time,
Sometimes thinks he's all mine.
My family never share him
And when they don't share him
I think he's made out of tin.
Don't think about it because I'm not selling him!

Leah Brown (11)
Measham CE Primary School

The Writer Of This Poem
(Based on 'The Writer Of This Poem' by Roger McGough)

The writer of this poem
Is as sweet as a rose,
As beautiful as a princess,
As stiff as a pose.

As white as a swan,
As graceful as Swan Lake,
As cold as ice,
As feathery as a drake.

As colourful as a rainbow,
As salty as the sea,
As small as a tadpole,
As far as I can see!

The writer of this poem
Drops down in a daze,
I think she's tired from running in a maze!

Abbey Lish (9)
Measham CE Primary School

The Wrinkly Queen

There was an old wrinkly queen,
Who fell in the washing machine,
She screamed out, 'Oh my,
I'm going to die,
But at least I'm going to be clean!'

Thomas Patrick (11)
Measham CE Primary School

The Writer Of This Poem
(Based on 'The Writer Of This Poem' by Roger McGough)

The writer of this poem
Is faster than a Ford,
As strong as triple glazing,
As clever as a lord.

As rough as Kilimanjaro,
As sour as can be,
As hot as a volcano,
As shifty as Tommy Lee.

As quick as thunder,
As smooth as a feather,
As heavy as a crane,
As hard as leather.

As tall as Robert Pershing Wadlow,
As posh as a Ford Cougar,
As talkative as Ben Thompson,
As deadly as Freddie Kruger.

Reiss Fielding (11)
Measham CE Primary School

There Was An Old Gentleman Of Crew

There was an old gentleman of Crewe,
He liked to row a canoe,
He toppled his boat
And started to float
That was the old gentleman of Crewe.

Adam Hollens (10)
Measham CE Primary School

The Writer Of This Poem
(Based on 'The Writer Of This Poem' by Roger McGough)

The writer of this poem
Is faster than a rocket,
As slick as a snake,
As deep as a pocket.

As sharp as a knife,
As clever as white room,
As clever as a doctor,
As quick as a bullet.

As smooth as an icicle,
As cool as an ice-cold lake,
As supportive as a floor,
As strong as an axe.

The writer of this poem
Never gets some laughs.
He's not one in a billion trillion
(Not what the poem says).

Jonathan Cobb (10)
Measham CE Primary School

The Writer Of This Poem
(Based on 'The Writer Of This Poem' by Roger McGough)

The writer of this poem
Is as small as a mouse
As beautiful as a mermaid
As safe as a house

As sharp as a skewer
As strong as a tree
As fast as lightning
As pretty as you and me

As funny as Mr T
As busy as a bee
As cunning as you and me
As calm as the sea

The writer of this poem
Is quicker than a tick
More gorgeous than my uncle Nick
(Or so the poem says).

Lauren Surch (11)
Measham CE Primary School

The Writer Of This Poem Is . . .
(Based on 'The Writer Of This Poem' by Roger McGough)

The writer of this poem is as
Colourful as a butterfly,
As keen as the north wind,
As cool as the one Clive.

As red as a rose,
As yellow as the sun,
As sticky as a cake,
As loving as my mum.

As bendy as a ruler,
As sharp as a pencil,
As cool as a book,
As strange as a stencil.

The writer of this poem is truly amazing,
But I think she's tired from a series of gazing.

Ellie Cashmore (11)
Measham CE Primary School

Swap? Sell? Small Adds Sell Fast!

1986 high speed brother
very rare like no other,
runs on pizza and Coke
and always cracks the same old joke,
which gets a little boring.

Hannah Bourne (10)
Measham CE Primary School

What's Happiness?

A row of bubbles circling around you,
A bright blue sky right above,
A shimmering sea with a silver top,
A hunormous yummy wedding cake,
A football cup,
A beautiful friendship bracelet,
A bluebell hanging from a vase,
A fragile mime of glistening gold,
A butterfly with spreading wings,
A clean bedroom,
A plate full of delicious food,
A star sparkling in the moonlight,
A smile on someone's face,
A sleepyhead full of dreams,
That's happiness!

Rhiannon Smallman (8)
Mickleover Primary School

What's Anger!

A sizzling plate of white hot chillies,
A lava spitting bursting volcano,
A catastrophic mad hatter,
A lion's ferocious roar,
A pair of jaws grinding their teeth,
The flashing speed of a rat pouncing,
The humungous size of the biggest giant,
The large bound of a dog,
The stink of rotten fish,
The huge bite of a tyrannosaurus rex,
That's anger!

Daniel Beddow (8)
Mickleover Primary School

My Naughty Little Sister

My little sister was sitting in the lounge,
She looked outside, guess what she saw?
A huge muddy puddle overflowing quickly,
She jumped up with a start, opening the French doors.

In the next minute or so she was right beside
The big muddy puddle and in she leapt!
But to her amazement she couldn't stomp around,
She fell down, right underneath the sticky slop.

She staggered out, sulking as usual,
But an idea struck her naughty brain!
She grabbed some mud, hid under a bush,
Waiting for me, *what a good plan*.
She thought!

I stood by the bush and out she jumped,
'Argh!' I screamed at the deafening, *'Boo!'*
We had a big mud fight, oh what a big mess,
I trudged in, grumpy, but she came in, chuckling!

Mum saw us and we were in trouble
But not just in trouble . . . *big trouble!*

Leonie King (9)
Mickleover Primary School

My Brother

He's blue with yellow stripes.
He's a kangaroo with a bouncing baby.
He's an autumn day with a lot of leaves.
He's a woolly hat with a pompom on the top.
He's an armchair that is cuddly and warm.
He's Power Rangers when he's in a bad mood.
He's lamb savoury with a lot of chips.

Thomas Robson (8)
Mickleover Primary School

My Little Brother

Me, brother, Mum and Dad,
Driving to the zoo,
Little brother said to me,
'I'm excited, are you?'

We were looking at the tigers,
When I had a scare.
Little brother had run away,
Little brother wasn't there!

We were furious,
Raging with anger,
'We haven't seen him!'
Protested the manager.

After looking near the lions,
Near the monkeys too,
From a bush leapt a little boy,
'I'm behind you! *Boo!*'

Alex Scrivener (9)
Mickleover Primary School

My Sister

My sister is yellow with purple stripes.
She's a puppy pouncing on a ball.
She's a sunny day at the beach.
She's a piece of armour when she's moody.
She's a hard, lumpy bed when she's horrible.
She's Tracey Beaker when she's mad.
She's spaghetti, Alphabites and chicken dippers
With tomato sauce.

Emily Reader (8)
Mickleover Primary School

If

If I were a pen I would write
kind letters to my friends.

If I were a pen I would write stories
that have happy endings.

If I were a pen I would write
sweet poetry to my family.

If I were a pen I would write
to my pen pals.

If I were a pen I would write
all about my feelings.

If I were a pen I would write thank you letters
to people who came to my party.

Georgie Barker (9)
Mickleover Primary School

What's Anger?

A bubble which never goes away
A piece of ash that burns the insides
A rush of passion that numbs the veins
A catastrophic hit of pain
A burst of water
A nightmare of ultimate stings
A stir of the blood
The bursting of the brain
A constant ringing in the eardrum.

Alexander James Suckling (8)
Mickleover Primary School

The Magic Glasses

Playing in the playground,
Screaming like mad;
When on the floor, Greg spied
A sparkling pair of glasses,
(And the plan was hatched.)

It would be funny if he swapped them for the teacher's!
Into Miss' case,
The swap was made.

Later on in class,
Greg sniggered at her appearance,
Startled, her glasses fell off.
'Gre,' she couldn't talk! *Hurray!*

Running in the playground,
This was the moment they had dreamed of,
She couldn't hear them or see them;
And that's why it was the best day they had ever had.

Guess what? Mrs Welder never knew!

Emma Shaw (9)
Mickleover Primary School

My Friend Chris

Chris is the colour blue.
He's an old cat resting all day.
He's a rainbow with bright colours.
He's great looking, cool and relaxed.
He's a bed with a comfortable duvet.
He's Woody Woodpecker with a funny laugh.
He's a McDonald's tasting just right.

Sam Aulsebrook (9)
Mickleover Primary School

What's Fear?

A large zombie knocks on your red bedroom door.
A lion jumps angrily on your back.
Get stuck in a room with hunting dogs.
A snake chops your hand off.
A cheetah knocks you in the muddy mud.
Fall into a boiling fire with a cat biting your big toe.
Fall into a blue sea with sharks and crocodiles in it.
Step into a room with sharks, crocodiles, zombies, lions,
Hunting dogs, cheetahs and big black cats.

Thomas Fletcher (8)
Mickleover Primary School

My Best Friend Lydia

Lydia is pink with purple stripes,
She's a puppy waiting to play,
She's a warm summer's day on the beach
She's a comfy cardigan that you wear when you need cheering up,
She's a nice cosy bed which you snuggle up to at night,
She's Coronation Street on the worst of days,
She's a Chinese dish served with pineapple on the side.

Alexandra Jayne Nelson (8)
Mickleover Primary School

Mrs Jones

Mrs Jones is orange with blue spots.
She's a pounding puppy chasing her hamster ball.
She's the sun shining on Lowestoft sea.
She's a pair of baggy joggers warn out to the bone.
She's as warm as my pillow.
She's as mad as The Simpsons in her funny way.
She's as crunchy as Frosties with no milk.

Harriet McDonnell (9)
Mickleover Primary School

A Light Bulb Dreams . . .

A light bulb dreams of being in David Beckham's room
And keeping him up
A light at the England rugby game when they won
A light at Big Ben when new year started
A light at the top of the Eiffel Tower
A light in Paul Scholes' bedroom
A light guiding boats to safety
A light at the pyramids helping people in the dark
A light at the Olympics and Paula Radcliffe.

Jamie Turner (9)
Mickleover Primary School

My Brother

My brother is black with a capital B
My brother is a guard dog with sharp teeth
My brother is a gale that blows you all over the place
My brother is a killer coat with a sharp zip
My brother is a hard chair with uncomfortable seating
My brother is the Bill with a nasty robber
My brother is a spicy curry but I love him.

Helen Perry (8)
Mickleover Primary School

My Sister Is . . .

My sister is bright pink with purple stripes
She's a little poodle curling her hair
She's a sunny day at the beach
She's a pair of green shorts with a yellow T-shirt
She's a fluffy sofa with soft cream fur
She's as The Simpsons when she has a drink
She's a nice McDonald's, I love to eat.

Natasha Payne (9)
Mickleover Primary School

A Shoe Dreams . . .

A shoe dreams of being a high heel shoe with gold laces on
Victoria Beckham's foot shining in the spotlight.

A shoe dreams of being a flip-flop on Britney Spears' foot
Under the beautiful, romantic, glistening sunset.

A shoe dreams of being on a tennis player's foot
On the Centre Court at Wimbledon.

A shoe dreams of being a fantastic mountain boot
Exploring the highest mountains.

Hannah Wagg (8)
Mickleover Primary School

My Brother

My brother is black with white stripes
He's a tiger with a very loud roar
He's the lightning of thunder
He's a pouffe that nobody wants to sit on
He's the Osbornes on a bad day
He's lettuce that nobody will eat.

Chris Mann (9)
Mickleover Primary School

If

If I was a snowstorm
I'd freeze the sun
Then cover all the cars and houses with ice
I'd freeze my two sisters
Make a blizzard with all my power
I'd cover the traffic lights
And snow with laughter.

Ryan Skidmore (9)
Mickleover Primary School

Shoe Dreams

A shoe dreams of being a football boot on Beckham scoring a goal.
A shoe dreams of being a flipper on a diver exploring the deep
dark ocean.
It dreams of being a high-heeled shoe on Victoria Beckham dancing.
It dreams of being a wellington splashing in puddles.
It dreams of being a skier's boot skiing in the snow.
A shoe dreams of being an ice skater doing a beautiful performance.
A shoe dreams of being a trainer in the Olympics.

Daniel Harrison (8)
Mickleover Primary School

My Mum

My mum is a peachy-pink colour with lively yellow stripes.
She's a tiny puppy asleep on a woolly scarf.
She's a summer's day that warms me up.
She's an old fleece jumper that I always like to wear.
She's like a warm cosy sofa that I snuggle up to when I'm ill.
She's like Coronation Street on her worst days.
She's like chocolate melting in my mouth.

Lydia Roworth (8)
Mickleover Primary School

My Mum

My mum is orange with yellow zigzags
She's a barking puppy chasing a cat
She's a sunny day in the middle of a desert
She's an old shirt that's been worn for years
She's a cosy armchair tattered and warn
She's 'You've Been Framed'
Because she's full of fun and laughter
She's pie and chips with gravy.

Katie Yeomans (8)
Mickleover Primary School

If

If I were a butterfly I would
tower above your head like a skyscraper.

If I were a butterfly I would
tug at your jumper to come and play with me.

If I were a butterfly I would
spread my pretty wings so you could see how beautiful I was.

If I were a butterfly I would
settle on a flower and collect the nectar to feed myself.

If I were a butterfly
I'd look into your bedroom window
and wake you up to see if you would be able to come out and play.

Laurie-Leigh Grainger (8)
Mickleover Primary School

If

If I were a clock,
I'd change time forward,
And wake people up late,
I'd make time go past home time
And then stop working.
I'd make more time to do homework
And make you stop up late.
If I were a clock,
I'd make no bedtime
And skip school
I'd never stop working
And go forward one hour by myself.

Luke Cheetham (8)
Mickleover Primary School

A Shoe Dreams . . .

A shoe dreams of being on David Beckham's foot
And scoring the winning goal for Real Madrid

A shoe dreams of being on a scuba-diver's foot
And exploring the crystal clear ocean.

A shoe dreams of being on the Queen's foot
When she makes an announcement to her people.

A shoe dreams of being on a tap dancer's foot
That dances merrily on the marble floor.

A shoe dreams of being a sandal in the shining sun
On the sandy beach.

Danny Cunningham (8)
Mickleover Primary School

Bonio The Brave Dog

The cat in the road
Was spied by the dog.
A car came speeding!
'Must save the cat.
Chase it.'

Crash, bang, yelp!
'Phone the vet.'

Brave dog
Saved cat.

Jessica Burman (9)
Mickleover Primary School

Supermarket Catastrophe

Supermarket shopping,
Little sis came too.
Sweets for me,
Fruit shopping for Mum.

> Oranges, bananas, mangoes and plums,
> So many choices,
> No time to keep an eye on Lily,
> No time at all.

At the till, *ping*,
No Lily.
Worries,
Cries.

> Racing around,
> Remains nowhere to be seen.
> What is she doing?
> Where could she be?

One to go,
Could she be there?
You naughty girl,
Where have you been?

> Tears of anger,
> Keep the tissues coming.
> Hugs and kisses,
> Huge smiles.

I get the punishment,
No fare. No fare!
Stomps of rage,
Howling screams.

> Guess what . . .?
> I have to babysit!

Amelia Draper (10)
Mickleover Primary School

My Baby Sister

I can't take it anymore!
She keeps me up all night,
She spits mashed potato like a cannonball.
She's a disgusting lump of goo!

I feel like a pile of dust,
Being blown away by that despicable baby.
In her hands, plasticine,
Squashed!

My mum and dad named her Daisy,
Which I think is totally pathetic and untrue,
For she is not a pretty flower,
She's a slimy toad!

She's playing in the sandpit,
She's building a sandman.
But it looks like two beach balls
On top of one another.

'Daisy,' I scream, 'I'll save you!'
I dive,
I hit,
I cry.

I still have the scar,
At least I saved Daisy.
She wasn't hurt,
Thankfully!

I love my baby sister,
She can be a bit of a pain,
But I know I'll never trade her,
She's a little statue of gold,
To me!

Evangeline Harvie (10)
Mickleover Primary School

Gruesome Grub

Frankie's mum bought him a cookery book,
He opened it up to take a look,
Inside he found the funniest makes,
From alien heads to creepy cakes.

He made a list of food to cook,
Into the kitchen now he snook,
A bowl, a spoon, some butter and flour,
Would it all be cooked in an hour?

Mixing, chopping, never stopping,
While Frankie's mum was busy shopping,
Dead man's hand: mmm how yummy,
Yeti's foot: he rubbed his tummy.

Out of the kitchen Frankie ran fast,
When hearing a scream, a shriek and a blast,
Cowering and trembling he peeped round the door,
And spotted big footprints on the floor.

From inside the oven a hand appeared,
Around the room, eyeballs careered,
Into the cupboard Frankie shot,
And slammed the door against the lot.

Home from Asda Frankie's mum came,
To find her son crying in shame,
She saw a burnt cake and Yeti's foot,
The dead man's hand was covered in soot.

I'm afraid to say from that day on,
Frankie didn't even cook a scone,
Mum had soon cleaned up the room,
With chocolate biscuits she cleared his gloom.

Edward Ody (9)
Mickleover Primary School

The Run

Shorts, T-shirts
No dresses or skirts,
Warm up quick,
We don't want to be sick.

We are all ready to run,
Come on it will be great fun.
We will all be full of joy,
As we scamper, both girls and boys.

Passing people,
Very fast,
We will not let
Anyone pass.

Trees and flowers
Are a blur.
As we run
As if on air.

The finish line
Is now in sight,
So reach for it
With all your might.

Emma Swindell (10)
Mickleover Primary School

What's Anger?

A screaming fire alarm
A red-hot bowl of lava
A bull about to attack the matador
A sizzling saucepan of hot fat
A bursting balloon
Blood dripping like a Ferrari through my veins
That's anger!

Tom Foster (8)
Mickleover Primary School

My First Ever Football Match

My first ever football match: so excited,
I can't wait to get on the pitch,
We start to train, feeling nervous,
Then my face falls: sub.

The match kicks off and we play well,
We have the ball in the box,
'Yeeesss!' we scream,
The keeper doesn't save the shot.

The goal gives us a giant boost,
But the player on the other team is clear,
We watch, hoping the keeper will save it,
But our hopes fade: it is 1-1.

Half-time
Will I be brought on?
On the pitch
I wish my nervous feeling would disappear.

I've got the ball,
Open goal,
I think it's going to end 2-1, the score.
It hits the net, *'Hooorrraaay!'*

Oh no, it's disallowed,
A free kick but no goal,
My excitement fades,
2-1.

Lewis Thomas (10)
Mickleover Primary School

We Went To Town

In the busy town,
Derby was alive.
Me, my mum, my little sister,
Looking for jeans.

'Go watch TV, Rach,'
Mum and I pleaded,
Happily she went,
'Finally alone,' we sighed.

Half an hour went by - no jeans,
Off we rushed,
No going home,
'Let's go to Marks and Spencer,' I suggested.

Getting there we saw them,
To the changing room we charged.
'Rach,' Mum screamed,
Rushing back.

Madly asking everyone,
One said, 'We sent her to Marks and Spencer,'
Rushing back to Marks and Spencer,
Would she be there?

She was!
'Give me a hug.'
'You silly billies,' Rach giggled,
'Sorry,' we cried.

Bethan Crocker (9)
Mickleover Primary School

Baghdad; The City Of War

Troops patrolling streets,
Looters steal,
It is like an envelope
That just won't seal.

Our lives in ruins,
Bombs, grenade attacks,
Senior officer dead,
And Saddam Hussein has fled.

No killing!
No violence!
Fires flare!
We want a fresh start, that is fair.

Helicopters targeted,
Houses invaded,
Since the war began
Our lives have been as rough as they can.

I want the aid that I deserve;
My son has poor health,
He will soon die,
We don't deserve it, so why?

Jenna Dunn (9)
Mickleover Primary School

My Mischievous Monster Brother

Bang, bang, bang!
The noise pierces my ears,
Big work machines crash outside,
How will I get any peace?

'Charlie, don't touch, OK!'
He gives a chuckle.
Builders and little brothers spell trouble,
Especially today anyway.

Scurrying down the huge hole,
Dodging big rocks,
He sees with his beady eyes,
Takes a step closer.

'Argh!'
Total silence,
My heart pounding,
Sprinting into the garden.

I grab the washing line,
Put it down the dirty hole,
Holding on to it tightly,
My brother also grabs hold.

'Yes, well done, Sis,' Charlie screams.

Ellie Joslin (10)
Mickleover Primary School

My Cousin James

The sun was out,
The sky was blue,
The sound of children laughing,
The calls of excited adults frantically shouting for their children.

The park was packed with crowds of people,
Including wailing James, me and George.
Our auntie said to get some bread
From the local shop.

'Go on George, buy the bread,'
As he dawdled
Fell behind,
Off he went, 50p in his hand.

'Come on James, let's get an ice cream,'
I said to stop him whining,
But there he stood, staring at the ducks,
'We'll come back this way,' I said patiently.

At the ice cream van,
The lady got impatient,
So I picked one for him,
One with a chocolate flake.

We walked beside the lake,
But . . . 'James, please keep away from the edge,'
But no, he paid no attention,
Dropped the chocolate flake in the lake.

'No James, there's no point,' I said
As he tried to fetch it out,
An accident waiting to happen.
'Oh no!' I screamed. I was right.

Off we went home
With our silly, soggy cousin, James.

May Worthington (9)
Mickleover Primary School

My Little Sister

My sister and I,
We share the same room.
And every night
Ends up in doom.

I sleep on the top bunk,
She sleeps on the bottom,
She thinks it's not fair,
She thinks I am rotten.

One day when I'd gone
To my friend's for tea,
She got into my bed
And pretended to be me.

I was so very cross,
I started to shout,
But she thought she was funny
And wouldn't get out.

I stropped around our bedroom,
I wasn't having fun,
And to make it even worse,
She had an iced bun.

I got into her bed,
And there was a treat,
There were crumbs spread all across
Her clean, white sheet.

I got up and I poured
Crumbs upon her head,
She was so very angry,
She jumped out of my bed.

Megan Aubeeluck-Davies (9)
Mickleover Primary School

Big Trouble

Supermarket:
Bored stiff,
'Do we have to look at girly shoes?'

Checkout:
Bored stiff,
Mum wandering away leaving us to pay.

Sister vanishes,
Should I follow?
Not more girly shops.

Earrings, clothes,
Bubble bath, chocs,
Fluffy toys and even more clothes.

Mum reappears,
Shouting like mad,
Everyone stares, how embarrassing is that?

Travelling home,
Fury versus silence,
I'm the silent onlooker.

'How much have you bought?'
About one hundred things,'
Mum doesn't react very well . . .

Sam Forrest (9)
Mickleover Primary School

Never Play On The Road

One sunny day,
Spikes came out to play,
He was sure of the road,
His wise friend, Toad
Had told him not to dare
Cross it.

His friend called Plumb
Was extremely dumb,
'Let's play on the road
And never mind that Toad.'

So they played on the road,
And forgot about Toad,
Heading for Plumb,
Was a driver drinking rum.
Plumb got a smack
Right in the back,
He was dead,
And off with his head.

What a poor bunny
And what a very lucky
Hedgehog.

Alex Brannan (10)
Mickleover Primary School

When I Lost My Mum

Huge over towering aisles,
Swirling all around me,
Too busy to watch over my mum,
I go twirling round looking at all the things to buy!

I turn round to find my mum,
But oh, where's she gone?
I squeeze past the people in front of me,
Suddenly something hits me on the head, *'Ouch.'*

Finally the end of the aisles,
I race around,
Of course she'll be there,
But no, my search continues.

Fast as I can to the help desk,
A message booms around the store,
I want my mum,
'Please,' I beg.

Sad and unhappy,
Unwanted and alone,
Panic rises inside me,
'Mrs T Bugg, come to the help desk!'

Looking around,
Jumping up and down,
Then I hear a familiar sound,
As Mum races towards me!

I've found her!

Natasha Bugg (10)
Mickleover Primary School

My Melting Masterpiece

On a winter's day,
Out in the garden,
Sitting down on a bench,
Deciding what to do.

I put my gloves on,
My hat,
My scarf,
I am ready:

I start to build,
I roll the enormous snowball
Into the perfect position,
Put head on body; nearly done!

Into the house,
In the fridge,
I search through: nuts, cake . . .
Ha, ha! Raisins and carrots.

Back outside,
Placing them on,
Pleased as punch
With my sculpture of ice.

Dinner time,
Hurrying, desperate to return.
'Mum, come here, look at . . .'
Puzzled, 'Why are there carrots and raisins on the lawn?'

Coral Hancox (9)
Mickleover Primary School

Mum Goes Missing

People shopping
Meanwhile I'm panicking
Where is Mum?
Where is my mum?

I'm looking around,
No one's there,
I'm running down the aisle panicking,
My heart's going *thud, thud!*

Every aisle I search
Looking for my mum,
Shoppers in my way,
My heart now faster, *thud, thud, thud!*

I see a Tesco worker,
I charge to him, relieved,
At the office
Nervously telling the manager.

The loudspeaker is on,
'Mrs Atkinson please report to the office,'
I am hoping,
Will she come?

I wait,
No one comes,
A phone call later,
I hear my mum's comforting voice!'

Lucy Atkinson (10)
Mickleover Primary School

Music Mayhem

Boring. It's Tuesday. Hymn practice.
My voice is like a cow's,
But my teacher (Miss Tank) is like twenty cows,
She's ginormous!

'If only Avril Lavigne would come,' my friend said.
The hall floor went still.
'Now Grade 5, let's sing 'Have you . . .' Miss Tank went quiet,
Even a cricket could be heard!

Suddenly the windows broke,
The silence smashed.
Miss Tank tiptoed towards the door.
Avril Lavigne and her gang leapt down from the sill.

Avril screamed, 'Get the fat one!'
And her gang shoved Miss Tank outside,
Locked the door.
'Now let's have some real music!'

The whole hall went bonkers;
We were singing, 'He was a Sk8er Boi' . . .
I volunteered for a solo,
I became Avril's helper. A helper!

Home time finally came.
Could I rewind and play?
No.
The smell of fresh air filled my nose.

The next day differed;
We learned rock music instead,
My mind flashed back to that day.
I would never forget the best day of my life.

Lucy Elliott (10)
Mickleover Primary School

The Ancient Scroll

Mum dragged me to the library that merry day,
She pushed and shouted but I wouldn't budge,
So she ended up dragging me instead,
But I really did not like that place.

'Get a book!' she said,
I searched and searched for the right type of book,
I shuffled and scurried in a hurry,
I found an ancient scroll.

From the scroll out popped a key
With directions to the tree,
I thought and thought when it suddenly hit me,
The tree in the park was the one for me.

I rushed and rushed as quick as could be,
To climb the massive tree,
In a crevice there was a book,
Shining brightly, just waiting for me.

The key I inserted to open the book,
Like a glove it fitted the lock,
But there ensued a flash of light
And I vanished out of sight.

Dominique Grocott (10)
Mickleover Primary School

I'm Lost

I scamper downstairs,
Put on my shoes
And we're off.

Chatting;
Talking;
Excited about the game.

Running to the game shop,
I find out that I'm lost,
I'm scared.

Running;
To the games,
I try to find my dad.

Squeezing, squishing,
Through people in my way,
I go to the escalator.

Looking round
I find my dad,
I hug him.

Driving home,
I wish I had not been so silly;
I'm never going shopping again.

George Hall (10)
Mickleover Primary School

The King Who Lost His Powers

Long, long ago,
animals ruled the world,
the monkey king with his magical powers,
carelessly lost his priceless gift.

A party went searching,
this way and that,
a shimmering, glistening lake
caught their eye.

Stumbling into the crocodile's lair,
getting ready to pounce,
snap!
And off with the king's head.

Croc used the head as a mask,
pretending he was king,
miraculously the king stumbled up,
made a master plan.

When croc was sleeping,
he stole his head,
croc was in the river,
still with the magic.

He claimed his throne,
and got a new head,
and went searching again,
he saw it in the river!

Stepping carefully,
the crocodile snapped,
but bumped his head,
then he grasped the magic and took off his steel head!

Josh Gahonia (9)
Mickleover Primary School

Hang-Gliding Accident!

One time my best friend went hang-gliding,
Gliding over Germany,
Hang-glider out of control,
Spiralling down,
Crashed to the floor.

Didn't know where he was,
Couldn't walk,
Screamed for help,
Nobody heard.
Feeling weak; thought he was going to pass out.

Heard footsteps, screaming, shouting,
Heart was pounding,
Saw shapes appearing,
Looked human,
But they weren't.

Fear in his eyes,
Praying for a miracle,
Crawling,
Hands sweating,
He saw them.

Disgusting, green, ugly.
Heard rumbling,
Tank in sight,
Missile flew out,
Field cleared.

Man appeared from tank,
'Sam'
Crawled to the tank.
Safe.

Ben Clarke (9)
Mickleover Primary School

Locked In The Workshop

It was dark,
Gloomy,
Not a sound,
Only drills and tools.

Surrounded by shadows,
Giant tools were making
Dragons, monsters,
Snakes and ghosts.

He found a hammer,
And whacked the door,
Did it work . . . ?
Not a chance.

He found some oil,
Squirt on the door,
So he could get a screwdriver
To let him free!

So that never worked.
But another one came,
He found a drill,
And made a chain.

He pulled the chain,
But then it snapped,
So he drilled the door down
With a *bang!*

A helicopter came,
He picked him up,
He flew back home,
In a rush!

Steven Cornforth (10)
Mickleover Primary School

Hang-Gliding

It was the worst day of my life,
I thought it was going to be good . . .
At first
But I was wrong . . .

We finally reached the centre,
Got on a hang-glider
Each, and before I knew it,
I was in the air!

At first I was relaxed,
With my hair whistling along behind me,
But all of a sudden -
Fear set in.

I imagined birds chasing me,
Pecking me,
Hurting me,
And then I returned to the real world.

All of a sudden,
I noticed something by the side of me,
A rope!
I carefully stretched out a hand . . .

Pulling and tugging,
I realised I was losing height,
Further and further, down I went,
'Argh!' I screamed.

I landed . . .
On top of an old lady finishing her shopping!
I ran for my life,
I'm never going gliding again!

Siân Grant (9)
Mickleover Primary School

The Snowman

Snow of the iciest falls,
Herds of classes 10 and 12 stampeding onto a snowy playground,
Yelling,
'Make it bigger, make it fatter, make it taller!'

Gleaming like a diamond bright,
Encrusted with snow in the night,
Yelling,
'Make it bigger, make it fatter, make it taller!'

Taller than a person now,
Only tallest reaches top,
Yelling,
'Make it bigger, make it fatter, make it taller!'

Come, put on clothes,
Give it arms and, of course, a face,
Yelling,
'Make it bigger, make it fatter, make it taller!'

Some kids come, pelt it down!
Now it's rubbish on the ground,
Yelling,
'Make it bigger, make it fatter, make it taller!' Now we can't . . .

We stare, glare,
A voice in the air!
'The snowmen come and go.'

One playtime, one snowman, gone. Erased . . into purest of air . . .

Susannah Barnard (9)
Mickleover Primary School

My Broken Arm

Late one balmy night,
Scooting
Boredom!
Shalom! Jenna thought.

We took it in turns,
Whoopee,
Jenna showed off,
I showed off more!

Round we scooted,
. . . Suddenly I landed on the ground,
Soon I felt a sharp pain,
Numb.

'Fetch someone,' I moaned,
It felt like ages,
Mum and Dad stared
Before helping.

The X-ray was cool!
An ambulance man,
Made something silly,
He blew up a rubber glove.

24.00
Terribly tired,
I lay there thinking,
Zzzzzz . . .

Restless night,
Eyes wide open,
Jenna's guilt,
What a disaster it's been!

Nicole Dunn (9)
Mickleover Primary School

My Annoying Brother

One normal day, on a trip to town,
My brother sulked and started to frown,
Slopped his tongue out, 'It's not fair!
I want to stay at home, not go there!'

We arrived at town, looked at drinks,
My brother turned, had a glance then a blink,
Blue Boom, it said, the best of all,
He took it, stole it and ran back to the mall.

My brother got home, in the house,
Ran upstairs with his new pet mouse,
Reached in his pocket, took out Big Blue,
Drank it and shouted, *'Yahoo!'*

He turned into an alien, tentacles and all,
Slimy, sloppy, all on the floor.
Five seconds later turned back again,
'Never drinking that again!'

The next morning, needing a drink,
He looked at Big Blue, had a think,
My brother drank it, all of it,
And turned back, it was permanent!

Jack Pritchard (10)
Mickleover Primary School

If

If I were a book
I would take people to magical places
I would dust my front cover
And make it inviting, so everyone
Would want to read me
I would excite and delight them
With powerful phrases
I would give them a scare when
They got to the climax
I would put them to sleep as they read me in bed.

Alec James (9)
Mickleover Primary School

Anaconda In The Amazon

Anaconda
was dark,
green and black.
Huge body,
sliding through dark waters.
Its body is ready
to squeeze.

Anaconda
was death,
stalks its prey,
then squeezes
it into the jaws
of death.

Nicholas Reed (10)
Redhill Primary School

Horse

Horse
With dun-coloured fur,
Runs round the field,
Galloping . . .
The ground shakes, it stamps
Then it stops . . .
Then gallops round again . . .
I felt her rough fur
Ground shakes . . .
It rears up like a motorbike in action . . .
It bucks . . .
Then gallops round again . . .
All is quiet
It breathes heavily.

Sophie Webster (9)
Redhill Primary School

Black Cat

Black cat,
Darker than the night sky.
Thin and hungry.
It leaps up onto the dustbin lid.
It rummages round the dustbin
Looking for food.

Black cat,
Sits in the alleyway.
Looking at a mouse
But the mouse is too fast.
Then all the lights go on
And the black cat goes silently
Back to its hiding place,
Until the next night . . .

Vanessa Radford (10)
Redhill Primary School

Tabby Cat

Tabby cat,
Black as charcoal,
Brown as mud,
Creeps about behind bushes,
Spots its prey,
Jumps in the air . . .
But a miss!
But then spots something different
And pounces on it
And gets a kill.
Dashes around wildly and excitedly.

Haydn Bowley (9)
Redhill Primary School

Monkey

Monkey,
he is brown as an oak tree,
fuzzy as a cat's hair,
eyes sly as a fox,
swinging, swaying,
across the tree,
fast as dynamite,
ready to pounce
on its prey.

Monkey
in deadly groups,
swamping the jungle,
scratching each other,
fighting for bananas,
single-handed he takes food
off other animals,
monkey swings, ah, ah, ah!

George Cant (9)
Redhill Primary School

Dog

All soft and fussy
Dribbling everywhere
He never brings balls back
And flicks food in the air
Black all over
He scuttles up to you and jumps
Then silently goes to sleep.

Kirsty Dakin (9)
Redhill Primary School

The Tabby Cat

The grey striped tabby cat lurks in the garden
Waiting for its playmate.
Its green, gleaming eyes search for food.
It crouches into the grass, its tiny ears listen,
It pounces actively on a bug.

The grey striped tabby cat comes inside,
Greedily waiting for its food.
It fusses around me with a very deep purr.

My fingers run through its soft fur,
Its long and white whiskers wriggle
As it settles to sleep like a baby.
Its dry, small nose rubs against its basket.

The tabby cat lazily sleeps,
Tomorrow the tabby cat will wake
And have a new adventure.

Amelia Fletcher-Jones (9)
Redhill Primary School

Ferret

Ferret
Dark death,
Arches back to look for prey,
Furry as a rough mattress,
It scoffs its food to the bone.

Ferret,
Warm hunter,
Warmer then, colder.

Ferret.

Tristan Foster (9)
Redhill Primary School

Mouse

Small, cold mouse,
always on the run.
Peeping behind a rock,
looking out for cats.
Watching, twitching, never off guard.

Mouse
timidly going in and out,
attempting to catch.
Scuttling up a garden path,
dashing into a bush.
Cold, wet feet slowly turning warm.
Glad to live another day.

Laura Clough (10)
Redhill Primary School

Tiger

Tiger prowls
through the jungle.
As he sneaks
with his tail up high
he is a crafty, huge animal.
His fur so ginger and bright
but his nose is soft and bristly.
A fierce animal with claws
as sharp as pins.
A vicious animal
tiger prowls once again.

Vanessa Emery (10)
Redhill Primary School

My Hamster

My hamster has red eyes,
They are very big.
They stare at me most of the time.
My hamster is brown.
Her hair is fluffy, very fluffy.
My hamster is called Sasha.
She is very cute.
My hamster is so big!
She is the size of a baby guinea pig!
My hamster has black eyes.
My hamster is grey.
My hamster is small.
My hamster is brown.

Holly-Robyn Hempell (7)
Redhill Primary School

My Kitten

Kitten,
Energetic runner,
Jumps all day as quiet as a mouse,
Black as charcoal,
Snow-white socks,
Plays all day inside, outside.

Kitten,
Cute and small,
Warm as a radiator,
Cuddly on my knee,
And smoother than me
And I really love him.

Jamie Fenwick (10)
Redhill Primary School

Dogs

Dogs are more vicious than a lion.
He finds his prey and goes for it as fast as lightning.
Dog loves cow bone and in a few seconds
The cow bone is gone.
He's as greedy as a pig
And he's as fast as a cheetah.
His favourite breakfast is Weetabix
And his favourite tea is rabbit from a hole.

Alex Miskow (9)
Redhill Primary School

Dog

My dog is . . .
Darker than ebony,
Faster than lightning.
Rammie is his name,
He isn't very frightening.
When my dad comes home
He leaps with joy,
All because he is our
      Little boy.

Coral Fitzhugh (9)
Redhill Primary School

My Rabbit

She likes to play with her ball.
She sits in her food bowl,
And kicks her bowl around in her hutch.
She likes to eat a lot and sleep a lot.
Her fur is warm, her ears are soft.

Jonathan Hatchett (10)
Redhill Primary School

There's A Rabbit

There's a rabbit at the bottom of the garden
And he's in a very bad mood.
There's a rabbit at the bottom of the garden
And he needs a lot more food!
He nibbles some straw,
Then nibbles some more,
Then I come out
And he has a good gnaw.
There's a rabbit at the bottom of the garden
And he's in a very bad mood!

Thomas Reed (7)
Redhill Primary School

Dustbin Men

Early in the morning,
Before you're quite awake,
Without the slightest warning,
The house begins to shake,
With a biff, bang-a-biff, bang, bash!
It's the dustbin men who begin to bang, crash!

Katie Levers (8)
Redhill Primary School

Tree

T is for the big oak tree.
R is for red, ripe apple.
E is for eating a yellow pear.
E is for enjoying a great picnic
   under a tree.

Brendan Hewitson (8)
Redhill Primary School

If I Had This What Would It Be Like?

If I had a swan, a swan, a swan
What would it be like?
It would be like a white snowdrop,
A white snowdrop,
A white snowdrop on a pond.
If I had a greenfinch, a greenfinch, a greenfinch
What would it be like?
A tree twisting and turning in the breeze.
If I had a fire, a fire, a fire,
What would it be like?
It would be like a wood
With a hundred colourful flowers.

Hayley Sherlock (7)
Redhill Primary School

Jumping In The Clouds

Jumping in the clouds
I think I'm dreaming.
I've been there once
It's very, very bouncy
And I went to see the sun,
It was too hot for everyone.

Thomas Morgan (8)
Redhill Primary School

The Dinosaur

I live in the house,
Of course!
I saw a door I haven't been in before,
I opened it
And I heard a scary *roar!*
  . . . Out came a huge dinosaur!

Henry Sharpe (7)
Redhill Primary School

The Castle

The castle is black
It's creepy inside
The staircase is steep
So keep to the side
Go into the dungeons
You will make a few friends
But the vampire is coming
So ruuuuunnnnnnn . . .
They're coming after you
They're right on your toes!
Run as fast as you can,
They're catching up.
Aaaarrrggghhh!
Oh it was only a dream.
No need to scream . . .

Jason McKenzie (8)
Redhill Primary School

Cake

One day I ate a cake
And then I saw a snowflake.
I watched it fall,
It was so small.

I wanted more snow,
So we could throw
Snowballs at each other,
Especially my big brother.

I would build a snowman,
As big as I can,
When the snow goes away
It will be a sad day.

Alex Woods (8)
Redhill Primary School

Darkness

Darkness is creepy,
I'm very sleepy.
Sometimes very chilling,
Or the wind is blowing.

Darkness is creepy,
I'm very sleepy.
On a Thursday night,
Not very bright.

Darkness is creepy,
I'm very sleepy,
A fox prowls around,
Underground,
Darkness is creepy,
I'm very sleepy.

Alex Brown (7)
Redhill Primary School

If I Ruled The World

If I ruled the world there would be no war,
Nothing else to fight for,
People will be friendly to each other,
Just like a sister and her brother.

If I ruled the world school would be,
Between the hours of twelve and three,
Children could go out and play,
Strangers would not take them away.

If I ruled the world it would be fun,
Just like a playground for everyone,
I might be dreaming but I'd like to say,
Maybe I will rule the world one day.

Eleanor Parry (8)
Redhill Primary School

Animals

A is for alligator, covered in scales.
N is for nuts that squirrels like to eat.
I is for inside where some pets are kept.
M is for mice that make the house creep.
A is for animals that this poem is about.
L is for lizard that is cold-blooded and a reptile.
S is for squirrels, some different colours, red and brown
This spells *animals*.

Hannah Sisson (7)
Redhill Primary School

Seasons

Spring is when we go 'ding'
Summer is when we say 'What a bummer'
Autumn is when we sort 'em
Winter is when we get a splinter.

Thomas Galloway (7)
Redhill Primary School

Trees

T is for trees.
R is for red crunchy leaves.
E is for enjoying all the rustling leaves.
E is for eating my lunch under the tree.
S is for stop! and let me be.

Benjamin Tennett (7)
Redhill Primary School

Cat's Car

Cat likes his car,
His colourful car,
Teddy likes it too,
It's pink and red and yellow and blue,
They go for a ride and you can come too,
Over the hills and faraway,
They can travel night and day.

Isabel Walters (7)
Redhill Primary School

A Stinky Feet Boy

There was once a boy called Pete,
Who had extremely smelly feet.
Everyone knew,
When he took off his shoe,
That stinky feet boy called Pete.

Vicky Horton (11)
Redhill Primary School

The Old Man From France

There was an old man from France
Who really loved to dance.
He fell on his bum
So he cried for his mum
That silly old man from France.

Emma Little (10)
Redhill Primary School

Weight Problems

There once was a lady called Miss Sinclair,
Who sat on a very old chair.
Her weight appeared,
So the chair disappeared,
That silly lady called Miss Sinclair.

Jade McKenzie (10)
Redhill Primary School

Never Eat With A Fork!

There was an old man from York,
Who ate everything up with a fork.
Soup was a disaster
And so was the pasta,
The silly old man from York!

Susan Frankish (11)
Redhill Primary School

Limerick

There was a young lady called Helen,
Who liked to eat watermelon.
She got in such a mess,
She spoilt her new dress,
That silly young lady called Helen.

Theodora Maguire (10)
Redhill Primary School

There Was A Young Man Called Dom

There was a young man called Dom
Who by accident swallowed a bomb
He blew up the next day
Everyone shouted, 'Hooray!'
That foolish young boy called Dom.

Ashley Smith (10)
Redhill Primary School

The Wig Pig

There once was a bald lady from York,
Who went on a very long walk,
She bought a magical wig
And turned into a pig,
That stupid bald lady from York.

James McKinnon (11)
Redhill Primary School

The Old Lady From France

There was an old lady from France
Who did a funny pop dance,
She did a little jig
And lost her wig.
That funny old lady from France.

Rosie Hunter (11)
Redhill Primary School

There Was A Young Lady Called Polly

There was a young lady called Polly,
Who swallowed her favourite dolly,
She chewed it up good,
Coughed up the hood,
That silly young lady called Polly.

Abigail Teflise (11)
Redhill Primary School

A Man From Aberdeen

There was an old man from Aberdeen,
Who liked to be very clean,
He fell in a puddle
And he was caught in a muddle,
That very dirty man from Aberdeen.

Tom Mills (10)
Redhill Primary School

Too Much Pork!

There was a young boy from York
Who ate too much crackly pork!
He turned into a pig,
Then started to dig,
That foolish boy from York!

Alex Baldwin (11)
Redhill Primary School

The Alphabet Of Pokémon!

A is for Articuno, wings cold as ice.
B is for Blastoise, who lives in paradise.
C is for Charizard, who breathes red-hot fire.
D is for Dewgong, when he swims his head is higher.
E is for Electrode, who looks like a ball.
F is for Flareon, that looks cute but could make a fire fall.
G is for Girafarig, whose tail has a face.
H is for Hariyama, whose punches could easily replace.
I is for Ivysaur, whose vine whip is strong.
J is for Jynx, who can make humans go wrong.
K is for Kadabra, who attacks with all his might.
L is for Ledyba, who flaps hard in flight.
M is for Moltres, wings burning bright.
N is for Natu, small but prepared to fight.
O is for Octillery, tentacles flopping.
P is for Pikachu, whose electric is shocking.
Q is for Quilava, with a fiery back.
R is for Rapidash, who stays carefully on track.
S is for Seviper, who has a poison tail.
T is for Teddiursa, who does not like to fail.
U is for Ursaring, who's like a big bear.
V is for Venusaur, who tries his best affair.
W is for Wailord, whose size is so great.
X is for Xatu, beware of your fate!
Y is for Yanma, sounds nothing like a harp
And Z is for Zapdos, wings all zappy and sharp.

Jenny Jones (8)
Redhill Primary School

A Man Called Pig

There once was a man called Pig,
He liked to do a dance called a jig,
He sat on a log,
He lost his dog,
That silly man called Pig.

Connor Hewitson (10)
Redhill Primary School

There Was An Old Man Of Torquay

There was an old man of Torquay
Who spent ten pounds on a Ferrari,
He went for a spin,
Crashed into a bin,
The poor old man from Torquay.

Shayne White (10)
Redhill Primary School

Am I In Love?

As I sit on the window sill,
I was crying because I was missing you,
Wishing I was with you,
Forever and always loving you.

I stared up to the clouds above,
Asking myself, am I in love?
As across the sky flew a big white dove,
With me saying is this what it is like
To be in love?

I sleep at night dreaming of you,
Hoping one day you would be here with me,
Watching people as they think I'm cuckoo,
Just because I'm in love with you.

I wake up and think of you
And do you feel the same way?
Worried if I told you what would you say,
Would you laugh and walk away?

But do you know I think of you night and day,
Well now you do, and just for the story
And so you get it right -
I love you!

Brogan Brown (10)
St George's CE Primary School, High Peak

Countryside

Tulips and buttercups all in a row,
When it will snow all the flowers won't grow.
Daisies and poppies, daffodils too,
All these flowers all for you.

Different types of berries, in mixed up bushes,
Summer dew like drops of blue on the pond's bulrushes.
Blackberries, strawberries, raspberries here,
They're all for you that's clear.

On the river bank pond lilies bloom,
In the glistening water where fishes swim and loom.
Trickling, splashing, reflecting the light,
I'll show you these on a misty night.

Doves and wrens fly in the sky,
Swans glide through the milky clouds so high.
Peacocks stare with colourful eyes,
This is going to be your surprise.

Squirrels chewing on hazelnuts,
They scamper up and down the trees,
In the coolish, windy breeze.
They will run away but still can't hide,
This is a poem of the countryside.

Joseph Ingham (11)
St George's CE Primary School, High Peak

Games

G ames are sometimes exercise
A nd are fun
M e and my friends can play
E ven if we're inside we can
S till play.

Joshua Clinton (9)
St George's CE Primary School, High Peak

Snow

Snow is bright and nice,
It's all white like rice.
Snow comes every year,
It's all clear.
Water freezes and icicles come,
Children are playing, no school just fun.
Animals are hibernating,
They come out in spring.
Snow is cold and soft,
People build snowmen,
Children are playing snowball fighting,
They come in with red cheeks and red noses,
But at least there's still tomorrow
There will be more good fun.

Natasha Spencer (10)
St George's CE Primary School, High Peak

Autumn

Falling leaves,
Denuded trees,
Ice-bound people,
Frozen steeple.

Coloured leaves,
Animals seen,
Jewelled grass,
Woolly hats.

Cloudy sky,
Frosty nigh,
Animals hibernate,
Some die.

Leanne Williamson (10)
St George's CE Primary School, High Peak

Horses Are Cool

H orses are big,
O striches are faster than Sophie,
R eally pretty Sophie,
S ophie the horse is going to a dance party,
E veryone will be going,
S ophie will be eating chocolate buns.

A nd be dressing up really fancy,
R ed shoes are her best ones,
E leven of her friends will be wearing a dress

C lear blue night just right for a dance party,
O f everyone in the crowd she looks the best,
O ver everyone at the dance Sophie will be
L ooking cool.

Megan Chatterton (10)
St George's CE Primary School, High Peak

Dog Sonnet

Shall I tell you about my friend?
He's small, black and grey,
He's smooth and woolly from top to end
And he always wants to play.
His name is Oscar,
He's not a cat
And he does not purr
Or sit on a mat.
He's up to my knees,
He's got a curly tail
And tries to sniff bees
And he's always on a trail.
I could squeeze him until he pops
Because I love my dog lots and lots.

Halana Mellor (11)
St George's CE Primary School, High Peak

My Cat Poem

M ad,
Y awning (always sleeping).

C heeky,
A ttention (she always has),
T oo much loving.

P urr,
O range and black,
E ating (she always eats),
M ischievious.

Hollie Maxwell (11)
St George's CE Primary School, High Peak

My Dog Kelly

My dog is called Kelly,
it looks like a lump of jelly,
it runs around the garden,
with its little round belly.

My dog is so cool
it can dive into a pool,
people say it is a fool,
but my dog is so cool!

Ryan Williams (10)
St George's CE Primary School, High Peak

Nothing But Worry

There was a young girl called Chloe,
Who was always in such a hurry,
She fell on her knees,
And said oh dear me,
And now she does nothing but worry.

Chloe Barton (11)
St George's CE Primary School, High Peak

Guinea Pig Haiku

Guinea pigs are great,
They are sweet and soft to touch,
I love them so much.

Andrew Wood (10)
St George's CE Primary School, High Peak

Mums

Mums deserve a large bouquet.
Mums tidy from Monday to Sunday.
Mums cook like a dream
And make yummy ice cream.

Mums chatter, Mums natter.
Mums think when they blink.
Mums drive us to school
And Brampton Manor's pool.

Tom Brown (9)
St Peter & St Paul School, Chesterfield

Where Does My Pencil Go?

Where does my pencil go?
It is on the floor and I didn't know.
Where does my pencil go?
It's in my bag and I didn't know.
Where does my pencil go?
It's on the desk and I didn't know.
Now my pencil doesn't run away
Because it's behaving better every day.

Alexander Hodgkinson (8)
St Peter & St Paul School, Chesterfield

Number One Pain

In my family there is one pain
It's not my sister Jane.
It's not my cousin Cathy,
Or my auntie Taffy.
It's not my uncle Dan,
Or my other cousin Fran.
It's not my grandma Milly,
Or my grandad Billy.
In my family there is one pain
And that pain is *me!*

Becky Hartshorn (9)
St Peter & St Paul School, Chesterfield

Hats

Tall hats,
Small hats,
Different colours red, green and blue,
Cosy hats,
Fun hats,
Such an assortment,
Difficult to choose.

Callum Howie (9)
St Peter & St Paul School, Chesterfield

Monsters

The monsters will come out to play,
Every single day,
They play football during the month of May,
After they have played football,
They will play dodgeball every other day.

Richard Berry (8)
St Peter & St Paul School, Chesterfield

Winter Is Coming

Crispy crunchy leaves,
The swishing sound of trees.
Squirrels jumping, foxes hunting
I feel the winter breeze.

Storm clouds are gathering,
Rolling in the skies.
Will it be rain or hail
Or sleet or snow?
Winter is here before my eyes.

Laura Singleton (8)
St Peter & St Paul School, Chesterfield

January

J umpers thick to keep us snug.
A lways remember a woolly scarf.
N ever leave the door open.
U nable to sunbathe, far too cold!
A nimals hibernating.
R ed cheeks and red noses.
Y oung children playing in the fresh air.

Bryony Price (9)
St Peter & St Paul School, Chesterfield

Places Where I Smile

I smile everywhere

I smile when eating sweets
I smile in my favourite shop
I smile while watching TV
I smile when I'm safe at home
I smile at school, in lessons too!

I smile whenever someone smiles at me.

Edward Richardson (8)
St Peter & St Paul School, Chesterfield

Who's That?

Who's that? It's Auntie Milly.
Who's that? It's me being silly.

Who's that under the table?
It's me, Suzannah reading a fable.

Don't forget cousin Jo.
He is always on the go.

And there's sister Jane.
She really is a pain.

There is my mum, jolly Molly
And her best friend Mrs Polly.

But my favourite person in the family
Is my dad, he is mad,
. . . He is mad about *me!*

Suzannah Hayes (9)
St Peter & St Paul School, Chesterfield

Books

Books books
Lovely books.
There are big ones and small ones
Short ones and long ones.

Books books
Lovely books.
There are fiction and fact books
Adventure and fairy tales.

Books books
Lovely books.
Myths, legends and fables
Piles high on wooden tables.
Lovely books.

James Davies (9)
St Peter & St Paul School, Chesterfield

I Don't Know Why?

My aunt has a big red house
I don't know why.
My aunt has a red, chubby cat
I don't know why.
My aunt wears a big red hat
I don't know why.

My aunt always wears red blusher on her face
I don't know why.
My aunt has a big red coat
I don't know why.
My aunt wears a big red gown
I don't know why.
My family says she is the best red person
I don't know why.
Everyone loves her, why don't I?
I don't know why.

Sabah Jadoon (9)
St Peter & St Paul School, Chesterfield

Sooty The Dragon

Sooty, Sooty he loves playing footy
but he is kind of nutty.

He scored for a day
we all shouted hooray!

But one problem he met
he stuck in the net.

Then he flew back home,
his house looks like a Millennium Dome.

He climbed up to his bed
and saw sleeping, his favourite ted.

His mum said, 'Sooty, night, night,
keep safe, sleep tight.'

Ryan Hinchliffe (9)
St Peter & St Paul School, Chesterfield

Lassie

My dog loves the sea,
She's as friendly as can be,
With a brain the size of a pea
Is my dog Lassie.

When she looks at me,
I feel inside, kind of wobbly
Lassie shows me lots of love
I know this, when she gives me a shove!

Katherine Parkin (9)
St Peter & St Paul School, Chesterfield

Daffodils

Daffodils are blowing my way,
I just sit there staring at them each day.
They're bright and yellow,
And when they're blowing
They sound like somebody is playing a cello.

Amber Richardson (8)
St Peter & St Paul School, Chesterfield

Space Impact

I'd love to go into space one day,
To see the sun, the moon and the stars.
I'd fly around from noon till night,
And probably end up on Mars!

Lewis Spencer (9)
St Peter & St Paul School, Chesterfield

Me

C hats a lot
H ates writing stories
A lways hungry
R uns slowly
L ikes lollipops
O therwise known as Miss Sunshine
T ries hard at school
T ends to joke
E ats a lot.

Charlotte . . . that's me!

Charlotte Thompson (9)
St Peter & St Paul School, Chesterfield

A Hairy Chest

Once there was a man who
Had a hairy chest.
His hair grew and grew
And poked through his worn out vest.
He brushed his hair all day and night,
To prevent giving the neighbours
A dreadful fright!

James Sharpe (8)
St Peter & St Paul School, Chesterfield

Poppies

Poppies in the poppy field
Red, black and yellow,
Poppies in the poppy field
Growing in the meadow,
Poppies in the poppy field
Drinking from the soil.

Katie Patrick (8)
St Peter & St Paul School, Chesterfield

My Aunt Zelda

I have an aunt Zelda
She is only 60
And she looks like a wrinkled pixie.

She always wears a purple top
And a matching swirly skirt,
Her favourite pearl necklace, hanging
From her rumpled neck.

She has a short bob of pink hair,
That makes you want to stare and stare,
With bright blue dancing eyes
Shaped like apples and rhubarb pies.

I think if you saw her
You would adore her!
Only joking!
So watch out!

Bethanie Twigg (9)
St Peter & St Paul School, Chesterfield

The Fresh Prince Of Tony Blair

When the boss had a baby, no one knew what to do.
It isn't a very kingly thing for the minister to do.
He called for the parliament to ask them for advice,
They told him a man having a baby isn't very nice!
The reporters soon discovered about the most bizarre news,
So along came the TV and all the camera crews.
Soon there was a riot, not good news you see,
So that's how the Prime Minister gave his only son to me!

Rowan Borchers (9)
St Peter & St Paul School, Chesterfield

Dragons

There are
Red dragons
Green dragons
Yellow dragons
Too.

They live in
Rocky caves
In smelly swamps
And in dark leafy woods
Too.

They eat and eat
A large amount of meat
Because they're carnivores
Including
Naughty children, ooooh!

Rebecca Bayliff (8)
St Peter & St Paul School, Chesterfield

Winter

Snowy
      Blowy
Wintry
      Frosty
Shivery
      Icy
Chilly
      Gusty
Windy
      Breezy
Draughty
      Nippy
Crispy
      Unfriendly
  Brrr.

Siân Carter (8)
St Peter & St Paul School, Chesterfield

The Zoo

I love to go to the zoo,
To see the jumping kangaroo,
The cheeky moneys who all say 'Boo!'
Lions and cuddly brown bears,
Are all sitting there,
Later I had a break,
Near the peaceful lake.

Gagan Shiralagi (7)
St Peter & St Paul School, Chesterfield

My Puppy Sherman

My puppy Sherman is fat
And he is afraid of the neighbour's cat.

He is simply the best,
As he trots off to the east and west.

My puppy Sherman is as lazy
As a daisy.

Laura Hattersley (9)
St Peter & St Paul School, Chesterfield

Jewel

My dog is cute,
My dog is soft,
My dog is a sister to me,
She's my protector, my friend,
Keeps me warm when the day ends,
I'm never alone.

Charlotte Adams (9)
St Peter & St Paul School, Chesterfield

In The Winter

I felt freezing in the winter, winter,
I felt freezing last month,
I saw a snowflake in the winter, winter,
I saw a snowflake hit the ground.
I made a snowman in the winter, winter,
I made a snowman in the snow.
I heard a robin in the winter, winter,
I heard a robin in the tree.
I gave out bread in the winter, winter,
I gave out bread for the birds.

Beth Wood (10)
St Werburgh's CE Primary School, Spondon

Winter

Winter, as magical as frost-covered leaves,
Glistening in the winter's night.
And I feel the shiver running up from my
Fingertips when I touch the ice.
Snow like the crunching of burnt toast
Crumbles in my hand,
When I step indoors, oh! The warmth, the pleasureness
Of being in a warm room with hot chocolate at my feet.

Christina-Mary Wilford (10)
St Werburgh's CE Primary School, Spondon

Winter

Snow is here,
Christmas is near,
Children getting colds, oh dear!

Children playing in the streets,
Christmas dinner with all the meats,
Everyone having lots of treats!

Lucy Siena (11)
St Werburgh's CE Primary School, Spondon

Winter

Winter is a snowfall
And playing with friends,
Slipping and sliding all about,
I like building snowmen and messing about.

Winter is the creatures looking for food,
And trying to keep warm,
Flying and landing all around,
I like robins because you only see them in winter.

Winter is the view that you can see,
And hearing all the screams from a snowball
Fight across the street,
I love to have a snowball fight with my friends.

Winter is hot chocolate running down your throat,
Your family coming to help with the snowman,
Do you know my dad's scared of snow?

Jade Hogan (11)
St Werburgh's CE Primary School, Spondon

Snow

Snow is as white as a sheep,
In some places it's very deep,
When you go out it makes you shiver,
So you have to go out if you've got a paper to deliver,
In the house it's nice and warm,
While outside a huge snowstorm,
In the streets there's a massive snow fight,
All pretending that they're knights,
So try not to get lost,
But beware of the freezing Jack Frost.

Ben Osborn (9)
St Werburgh's CE Primary School, Spondon

Snowboarding

One day I went snowboarding,
And experienced a lot.
Because as soon as I got on the board,
I almost fell straight off.

Finally I caught my balance,
And slid right down the hill,
But then I fell right off the board,
And broke two of my ribs.

The next morning in hospital,
The nurse was really nice,
Although the night before I came,
I was as cold as ice.

After going snowboarding,
I've learnt not to go again,
Because the last time I went snowboarding,
I broke two of my ribs.

Joseph Cunningham (10)
St Werburgh's CE Primary School, Spondon

What Makes Winter?

Snowflakes splutter like frosted rings,
They spin and twirl in the wind.
The golden pearled sun glows down on the Earth,
Watching the snowland that God has created.

Trees so bare,
Skies so grey.
The winter moon is held in the sky,
Then the dark of night comes early.

Classroom windows sprinkled with snow,
They soon become frozen and solid.
All the fields are decorated with ice
And the roofs are dusty with sleet.

Sophie Ford (9)
St Werburgh's CE Primary School, Spondon

Mr Snowman

Here is Mr Snowman,
All dressed in white,
With a scarf around his neck,
He sure looks warm tonight.

In the garden standing,
By the pond he is,
One small step to the left,
And wet his scarf will be.

Next day he is melting,
From the sun up high,
I don't know if he'll be right there,
By the fall of night.

He won't be here tomorrow,
If he's melting here right now,
I'd better sing a goodbye song,
Or else he'll start a row.

Catherine Harper (10)
St Werburgh's CE Primary School, Spondon

Snow Wonderland

Snow is like falling stars in the sky.
Snow is like sweet cotton candy from the fair.
Snow is like the little shiny sugar crystals.
Snow is as cold as ice cream
And snow is as frozen as ice.
Snow is shaped in little balls
When someone throws it.
Snow is just plain shiny white.
When snow falls down it feels like it's tickling you
When you don't know it.
Snow is as slippery as being in water.
When snow hits it smashes and cracks into your face
Because snow is my wonderland.

Terry Ashley (11)
St Werburgh's CE Primary School, Spondon

Snow Day

When it's a snow day
Snow falls from the elegant skies above,
Like buds of cotton wool
That float slowly down
To the white covered earth.

When it's a snow day
The sun goes in behind
The ice cream puffy clouds
That float across the skies.

When it's a snow day
Snow will fall like tears
Rolling down a weeping face.
With the sun behind them
Leaving a glint in our eyes.

When it's a snow day
People hope the cotton bud-like snow
Will come again the next day.
So again it will be a *snow day!*

Bethan Hall (9)
St Werburgh's CE Primary School, Spondon

Snow Poem

Snow is white like cotton wool,
Snow is nice,
Snow is fun because you can throw snowballs,
But sometimes it can make you slip!
You can ride on your sleigh on snow
Snow you can jump in,
Snow is like a little light,
Like a star in the night.

Charlotte Eastwood (10)
St Werburgh's CE Primary School, Spondon

Winter Wonderland

Wouldn't you love a winter wonderland,
where the ground looks like candyfloss
and feels like fluffy cotton wool.

Wouldn't you love a winter wonderland,
where the soft foam padding catches you
when you fall.

Wouldn't you love a winter wonderland,
you could have huge snowball fights
all day long.

Wouldn't you love a winter wonderland,
you could build a massive snowman, called Fred
that touches the stars.

Wouldn't you love a winter wonderland?

I would.

Jessica Holyoake (10)
St Werburgh's CE Primary School, Spondon

Snow Poem

Children skidding along the ice.
Snowballs zooming across the street.
Wind blowing the frosted trees.
Snowmen standing in a field of snow.
Ponds and rivers frozen still.
The snow on the road is like a white sheet.
Snow falling from the cold winter sky.
Parks full of children playing snowball fights
And people inside by the fire drinking hot chocolate.

Luke Sumpter (10)
St Werburgh's CE Primary School, Spondon

Winter Pixies

As I look out of the window
I see trees that are iced with white delicate snow,
As if someone's decorated the trees with pure white icing sugar.

As I step out of the door
Something ice-cold lands on my nose,
And as I look up I see shiny crystals floating from the sky.

As I walk along the icy path
I slip and fall down on my bum,
And as I feel around, the snow is like fluffy white candyfloss.

As I step up and brush the remaining snow off me
I think to myself it's like a magical dream,
Overnight the winter pixies must have come and
                                      painted the world ice-white.

Nicol Winfield (11)
St Werburgh's CE Primary School, Spondon

Winter Days

When it has been snowing,
it looks like the world has been coloured in white.
It looks like someone has tipped
pure, skimmed milk over the earth.
It tastes of creamy, sticky candyfloss
Mixed into creamy ice cream.

When it has been frosty,
it looks as if a mirror has covered the whole world,
so slippy, skiddy and ice-cold.
Children love it when it snows or is frosty.
When summer awakes all that snow and frost
has gone away for another year or more.

Rebecca Bonsall (10)
St Werburgh's CE Primary School, Spondon

Winter

Dark, murky mountains clawing up at the crystal clear sky.
Water trickling down the long, rough icicle onto people's cold heads.
Ice glinting up at the sides of people's feet as they walk.
Frost covering everywhere like nail polish drifting
                              along a girl's fingernails.
Ducks quacking at the lake as if to say 'I want to swim'.
Snow as white as a blank piece of paper, not been touched at all.
Then, sadly spring comes and sweeps it all away.

Thomas Cornfield (11)
St Werburgh's CE Primary School, Spondon

Frosted Hands

When I go to play in the snow,
My hands go cold and numb,
Sometimes they feel as if they've vanished,
They feel as if they've gone,
They feel as if they've gone to The Netherlands,
It really can't be done,
It is a big mystery,
But I should tell you now
I think they really are there.

Emma Newman (10)
St Werburgh's CE Primary School, Spondon

Winter Garden

My winter garden is covered in white,
My winter garden has not a flower in sight,
My winter garden sees birds taking flight,
My winter garden sees them out of sight,
This is my winter garden,
Which I see at night.

Mark Harrison (9)
St Werburgh's CE Primary School, Spondon

Friendship Is . . .

Friendship is an invisible scene,
friendship is a spectacular dream.
Friendship is someone who is always there,
friendship is a friend who is kind and cares.

Friendship is great fun with your mates,
friendship is not someone who takes.
Friendship is a happy smile,
friendship is a bond that lasts for more than a while.

Friendship is a joyful cheer,
friendship is the fall of a happy tear.
Friendship isn't a sobbing nose
and that is how my poem goes.

Rachel Evans (11)
St Werburgh's CE Primary School, Spondon

Snowfall

Snow is falling from the sky
like a weeping child.
It is like the world has been
coloured in white.
It is like a sheet of wool.
You have icicles growing everywhere,
you can see them on trees, roofs,
Window sills, plant pots and things like that.
You can see it everywhere you go.
Snow is where you can go and play.

Paige Bray (10)
St Werburgh's CE Primary School, Spondon

Scooby The Dog

Lots of dog types, including Dalmatian,
But the type I have is an Alsatian.

I sometimes give him a hug,
Then he goes into the lounge and lies on the rug.

Scooby the dog's a friendly chappie,
When I come home he wags his tail because he's happy.

He likes to go for walks,
When he barks I think he talks.

Dad goes out to give him a fight,
But it ends when Scooby starts to bite.

Sometimes he's cheerful, sometimes he's sad,
Sometimes he's happy, sometimes he's mad.

When the postman comes he rushes to the door,
He grabs hold of the letters, throws them to the floor.

Matthew Cort (10)
St Wystan's School, Repton

Warg Riders

Warg riders have long sharp fangs,
They ride around in great big gangs.

They are armoured and carry shields,
Each has a battle sword to wield.

Orcs are creatures that are vile and vast,
Created thousands of years in the past.

They are squat, bow-legged and fierce,
With long muscular arms and eyes that pierce.

Driven to wreck, destruction wherever they can,
Avoiding the sunlight and hunting down man.

Orcs are commanded by Saruman,
He is desperate to conquer all of Rohan.

Callum McLean (9)
St Wystan's School, Repton

Titan Space Slug

It survives well in the vacuum of space,
No one can see its terrible face.

Impossibly gigantic, surviving all wars,
On fleeing starships he closes his jaws.

His head, a large temple-sized mound,
Antique blast scars from an imperial pound.

With one metre teeth how can it hide,
The Mynocks inside will be your guide.

This creature lives on a roaring comet,
Flying through space like a powerful rocket.

He leaps out like a blast of gas,
Then shoots back like an arrow whizzing past!

It's home, a hovel inside a rugged canyon,
He is very lonely and waits for a companion.

Thomas Jones (10)
St Wystan's School, Repton

Mumakil

The mumakil has grey leathery skin,
They are ridden by members of the Haradrim.

They destroy everything in their way,
Destroying trees is pure child's play.

Swinging and swooshing their tusks,
They sound their attacking cry at dusk.

On their backs sit great war towers,
Haradrim send out arrows in showers.

They head into the midst of the battle,
Trampling, crashing all they tackle.

They were in the battle for Middle Earth,
Their huge tusks grinding up the turf.

Robert Egan (10)
St Wystan's School, Repton

Prince

Prince the horse has ears long and tall,
A tummy as big as the Berlin Wall.

His coat is a shining summer's day,
His feet galloping showing him the way.

His eyes are as black as night,
His white mark shining bright.

His tail swishes left and right,
His mane flashing in the night.

His legs are muscular and strong,
Built to carry a passenger along.

His coat is oh so soft and warm,
Fit to survive even a lightning storm.

He meets some horses on his way,
Galloping softly on the summer's day.

Jessica Storey (9)
St Wystan's School, Repton

My Rabbit Lilly

Her coat is a spotty black and white,
She would never ever bite.

She has a butterfly nose,
Meeting lots of rabbits wherever she goes.

I love my rabbit Lilly so much,
And she lives with me in a wooden hutch.

She likes to eat my mummy's veg,
And sometimes escapes through a hole in the hedge.

She has the biggest teeth you could ever see,
Sometimes she even frightens me!

She is the best rabbit in the world,
Her fluffy tail is all curled.

Aimee Holder-Spinks (9)
St Wystan's School, Repton

Two Little Kittens

Two little kittens all soft and fluffy,
Sitting there all cute and cuddly.

They're both perched at different heights,
They're big round eyes gleaming and bright.

Two little noses all round and pink,
Their whiskers are long without a kink.

Their ears are pricked up and hear every sound,
If you wake them they're up with a bound.

They jump around the house ripping things to bits,
Sending their owners in crazy, mad fits.

They have feather duster tails which they swish with glee,
They have favourite food, chicken and tuna for tea.

Their teeth are sharp even though they are small,
They play fight together and tumble and fall.

Sophie Donoghue (10)
St Wystan's School, Repton

Chunky The Monkey

Chunky the monkey was an old fellow,
With a coat of banana colour yellow.

The monkey was related to a baboon,
And howls out loud when it's a full round moon.

He has long, soft and furry, fluffy skin,
Like a hot desert snake his tail is thin.

His piercing cobalt eyes sparkling bright,
His fierce red mouth, always ready to bite.

Chunky's tiny claws are as thin as rice,
Scratching fur and catching creatures like lice.

Chunky the monkey lives in the tall trees,
Happily swinging around with carefree ease.

Oliver Richards (9)
St Wystan's School, Repton

The Rattlesnake

The rattlesnake is as long as a truck,
He eats his enemy in one suck.

His scaly back is as rough as a stone,
His killing poison will chill anyone to the bone.

He gobbles frogs whole with his enormous jaws,
His deadly fangs are as sharp as saws.

He hisses loudly as he slithers through the night,
Searching for a warm soft throat to bite.

His yellow eyes will give you a fright,
He beats his rattle with all his might.

He sidewinds wavily through the grass,
Not even a rhino dares to pass.

His dark tail swishes with a long glide,
Dragging his dead dinner by his side!

David Chandler (10)
St Wystan's School, Repton

Kittens

The kitten's fur is as black as night,
His little eyes are sparkling bright.

Teeth so sharp, like prongs of a fork,
Ears that prick up when he walks.

Some are friendly and some are sweet,
They jump on your lap as if it's a seat.

He squints his eyes which are gleaming green,
Sometimes he can be fierce and mean.

He creeps through the night without a sound,
As quiet as a mouse, he's homeward bound.

His claws are thin but as sharp as pins,
Prowling around he'll scavenge through bins.

This cat is handsome and striking,
An animal mix of magic and lightning.

Holly Twells (10)
St Wystan's School, Repton

Eligah The Tiger

Eligah the tiger has teeth like steel,
He prowls through the jungle in search of a meal.

His huge orange body is covered in stripes,
He blends into the sky, on cold grey nights.

His long orange tail swings around,
His great loud roar makes a terrible sound.

His large arched back is three metres long,
He laps up a stream with a lick of his tongue.

His massive black claws stick out of his feet,
He stays in the jungle to keep out of the heat.

He can eat a whole zebra in ten seconds flat,
Every animal thinks he's the king of the cats.

Eligah the tiger is by far the best of his pride,
His reign in the jungle stretches far and wide!

William Barnett (9)
St Wystan's School, Repton

Rosie My Dog

A furry blanket warms the skin,
The pearly eyes are rather dim.

A long cream tail wriggles and swerves,
Her back is flat but her tummy curves.

She has a bubble bath now and again,
The water drips off her like falling rain.

She answers the call of each other dog,
She easily climbs over each stone and log.

She prowls around the house at night,
Making sure we are alright.

Although she's blind she's never sad,
She's by far the best dog I've ever had.

She's loving and kind in every way,
Each night in bed she dreams of play.

Emily Hammond (10)
St Wystan's School, Repton

Gollum

He has a rough and scaly skin,
To describe him, it's hard to begin.

His eyes are all red and bloodshot,
Like fiery coals glowing super hot.

His hair is all greasy and grey
He hides in his cave as he hates the day.

He once walked as a man among men,
Until he felt the urge to kill one of them.

But he couldn't resist the golden ring,
Men still try to kill this savage thing.

He whines and whimpers a withering cry,
Being watched all the time by Sauron's eye!

He follows the ring wherever it goes,
The power it has over him nobody knows!

Richard Gidlow (9)
St Wystan's School, Repton

Kiy Kay

Kiy Kay the cheetah has terrible claws,
Like sharp knives on the end of her paws.

She prowls in the jungle high on her heels,
Looking for large and tasty meals.

She has small laser piercing eyes,
She hunts all night until sunrise.

She moves her legs very fast,
Her body is so big and vast.

Silently she runs through the grass,
A dangerous cat to get past.

She watches her cubs high in a tree,
She sees them playing happy with glee.

Her whiskers cover up most of her face,
Carefully she watches over her race.

Victor Scattergood (10)
St Wystan's School, Repton

My Pet Spino

Spino is my pet dinosaur,
Please don't annoy him or he will roar.

My Egyptian lizard has teeth sharp and small,
His smile is so nasty it frightens us all.

His crocodile mouth rips red flesh,
His jaws open and close with a crash.

He has a long whippy tail,
And a crest on his back like a sail.

This angry beast is like no other,
When you see him it will make a shudder.

My spinosaurus is very brave,
Sometimes he will misbehave.

He can move fast on all fours,
He is the best of dinosaurs.

Tristan Griffiths (9)
St Wystan's School, Repton

The Porcupine

Her nose is very pink,
Her eyes are as black as ink.

Her whiskers surround her nose,
Guiding her wherever she goes.

Her really tiny ears stick out,
She can barely hear a shout.

Her spines are black and white,
They are a really scary sight!

Her barb-covered tail,
Is sure to make you quail.

She travels through the grass,
Patiently plodding, not very fast.

She is a spiky porcupine,
Steer clear and you will be fine!

Benedict Cross (9)
St Wystan's School, Repton

A Rose

An elegant beauty,
Yet cursed by the thorns that surround it,
Sweet-scented like love in many ways,
Tempted by water,
To drink, such a pleasure,
As red as spilt blood,
Pray no more shall be lost,
A perfect statue standing completely still,
In all its excellence,
The unique petals wouldn't miss the sun for anything,
For all to stop and stare,
A rose.

Naomi Dodds (11)
South Darley CE Primary School

The Sea's Life

The sea is home to many,
Crashing, lashing waves,
The fishes go down and down like a tossed penny,
The rocky bay stands quietly,
As the salty sea is lapping off and on it.

And the sea birds sing,
When the sea is unhappy it lives wildly,
The flowing of its life brings in tiny precious things,
When the people walk along, the sea is relaxing and sweet,
As the shark collects its meat.

The sea is calling me with its soft, pleasant lashing,
The clear sea is watching me even though it's far away,
With the flat fish swerving in and out `of the seaweed dashing,
I can taste the salty seaweed flying its arms about,
And the fishermen catching trout.

I wish I was with the fishes like I used to be,
With the clear sea and the swell breeze floating on my face,
The sea has every little fish and that is how it should be,
It has treasures and glistening things,
And the treasures have more for the sea and more they will bring.

Holly Ibbotson (9)
South Darley CE Primary School

My Torn Heart

We played a game,
Oh how I remember
The joyous times we spent together,
With the times we had, it felt so short
But strong with the time of love we had,
The love we had,
The love you gave,
You were my hero,
You were my friend.

I stand at a stone,
I stand at a grave,
I stand at a body that once loved me,
But why was it you?
I do not know,
The love we had,
The love you gave,
You were my hero,
You were my friend.

As I go my heart is torn,
But I always knew you were my man.
Goodbye, goodbye,
My hero,
My friend.

Emily Rathbone (10)
South Darley CE Primary School

Sea Trip

The sea is smooth and misty,
The fish are big and strong,
Tidal waves are roaring at the little ships sailing.
Seas are salty and glittering calmly on the gritty sand,
The sea is clear as the open sky
And the sea is as blue as bluebells swaying in the breeze,
Flowing up the rough, sandy beach,
Glowing in the moonlight like fire,
Star glinting lonely in the cold sky.

The melting salt is hissing,
The evil shark is killing,
The stormy waves are wrecking,
Baby crabs are pinching, baby fish swimming,
Dolphins are jumping from side to side,
Popping abandoned rubber rings,
That float, deflated to the sand of the rocky beach.

Ryan McClean (9)
South Darley CE Primary School

The Man I Love

Deep under the earth you sleep,
As I sit on the grass I weep.
My love for you is true,
I know I shall never forget you.

You have broken my fragile heart,
Since we got torn apart.
Thinking of you brings tears to my eyes,
I think of you from when I lie down and rise.

As I walk down your home street,
My eyes and your cottage still meet.
Your laughter I hear,
It feels like you're near.

Katherine Holmes (11)
South Darley CE Primary School

Death Departs

You are ill and I am well,
Our love is strong, stronger than ever now,
We shall not split,
I will not forget you.

Can I help you?
Can I help that you are ill?
I will love you,
I will love you forever.

You will suffer no more,
The world will go on,
It will go on without you,
And I will love you!

Your eyes glisten,
They shine like stars,
You are beautiful,
I will love you till death departs us.

Clare Harrison (10)
South Darley CE Primary School

The Last Kiss!

While you are lying there
My love will never leave the air,
Just because you have gone
It doesn't mean you're not the one.

I cannot forgive myself
Now you have no health,
Why couldn't it have been me
To be taken so suddenly?

I won't wash your last kiss away,
I'll remember you every day!

Maddy Sixsmith (10)
South Darley CE Primary School

Winter

Snow falling across a cold, bleak landscape,
Ice covers lakes and ponds,
Mother birds searching in vain for a scrap
Of food to feed their young,
A vicious wind whistling in the trees,
The whole world transformed into a white desert.

Then the snow stops,
Children come out to play,
Woolly hats, scarves and gloves
To keep the wind at bay,
Sledges, snowmen, snowball fights,
All fun to play,
But when the storm starts again
The children run away.

George Devereaux Evans (10)
South Darley CE Primary School

My Pet

Even now I'm still in tears
But you did live seventeen years.

Back in your happy, joyful days
You were strong and playful in many ways.

You bounced along across the grass,
I would love to have you back.

You were my special pet,
'She is ill,' said the vet.

When you died I was not there,
you died and I really do care.

You are happy now but I just can't see
That you are resting,
Resting in peace.

Emily Barrow (11)
South Darley CE Primary School

The Storm In The Sea

The sea is calling me
With its thundering roar.
I have to see the sea
With its clashing waves.

The sea is the rebel of the world,
It does what it likes whenever it wants.
It may be stormy when you're there,
It may be bumpy, uneven and wild.

The sea is tough and rough,
The sea is strong and bold,
The sea is crazy and mad,
The sea is choppy and sturdy.

The sea has a maze on the bottom of the bed,
The maze is stones and shells
Taken from the shore,
Oh how the sea is calling, oh how the sea is calling.

Daisy Rathbone (9)
South Darley CE Primary School

Winter

Woolly hats and welly boots,
It's cold outside but I must go out
To see the bikes paper-white.
The frozen and slippy ice,
A snowman with a tie and hat,
A sugary ball in the grass.
Children run out from their class,
They come out with their backpacks.
Snowy white they leave their tracks,
Run into the park and up the hill,
The children think the snow is brill.
It goes dark in the park,
They hope the snow will come again, some day.

Bethany Allwright (9)
South Darley CE Primary School

My Little Boat

Steering my little boat out of the harbour
Into the huge wide sea,
The sun shining in my eyes,
The sea calm and smooth,
Gentle waves lapping at the side of my little boat.

Thunder in the distance,
The waves get rough and vicious,
Trying to pull me under,
Roaring in my ears,
I pray to God in my little boat.

Suddenly I'm safe, my prayer has been answered,
The sea turns peaceful,
My boat sails rocking on the splashing waves,
Glistening and sparkling in the bright, golden sun,
They catch the gentle breeze, the sails of my little boat.

Land in sight,
My destiny is fulfilled,
I have finished my voyage,
I am still in one piece,
I step out of my little boat.

My little boat.

Alice Rathbone (10)
South Darley CE Primary School

Winter

Winter is the white season,
It turns lakes into cakes,
Everywhere there's tiny flakes,
Children sliding,
Black ice frightening,
Snowballs being made today,
They're being thrown in every way,
Winter makes the world white,
But when you wake up you may have a fright,
The snow gets turned into slush,
We're sorry when it's only mush.

Jordan Bullen (9)
South Darley CE Primary School

A Potion

Mix a potion full of lard,
Get a shining star,
Put in a bird's head and a bleeding bear's leg,
Put it in a shell,
Mix it very well.
Drink it up nice and quick,
Don't be sick.

You have one eye bigger than the other,
You turn into the worst mother.
You go all scaly white,
You are a dreadful sight.
You look in the mirror, you have toes
Growing out of your nose.
Your mind whizzes round,
Your cheeks blow up.
Your hair stands up just like some grass,
The you you knew you know no more.

Tom Hardwick-Allan (7)
Thornsett Primary School

I Wish . . .

I wish I could drive a fast car
And win a lot of races.

I wish I could be a footballer
And score a lot of goals.

I wish I had a cyclops
And could scare everyone in school.

I wish I was a sword fighter
And have good plans.

I wish I had a motorbike
And could ride every day.

I wish I was an astronaut
And go all round Mars.

I wish I was a dragon
And flew to a castle.

I wish I was a knight
And killed all the baddies.

I wish I was a vampire
And lived in a haunted house.

I wish I had a rabbit
And could play with it.

Max Bradwell (8)
Thornsett Primary School

Ponies

When I ride
I have some pride.
Crispy, Ivan, Mel or Bill,
Just gives me a thrill.
Magic, Milly, Merlin or Snowy
Makes me feel so cosy.
Snowy might be bad
But I still love him
So go on call me mad.
Toffee, Jett, Bailey or Merlin 2,
Not too good for you.
Bailey fast.
Toffee as fast as a bullet.
Plank or Merlin 3
Are just not me.
Now we will go back in time not seeing any pride.
Rambo, Paly, Honey or Jake
Are not good mates.
Fraggle got me in a mangle.
Further back in time we go.
I rode Gizmo up a hill onto the moor,
He dumped me there
So I tore after him onto the road
And down the hill.
But my number one horse was my mum's chestnut horse, Travis.

Katrina Cullen (8)
Thornsett Primary School

A Scary Poem

Once a boy stayed up very late
but he did not know
He was about to meet his fate . . .
So he turned off the TV and the DVD.
He went into the kitchen
And saw a shadow of a witch
Which turned out to be his cat,
He got tapped
On his shoulder . . .
He turned round,
Nothing was there
So he climbed the stairs
And got in bed
And wrapped up into a ball.

The wall shattered and a monster came through,
That was the end of the tale for Jonney Magoo.

Taylor Jones (9)
Thornsett Primary School

I Am A Fish

I wish I was a fish
I'd swim all over the sea,
I'd dodge past the sharks,
Make sure I didn't get hurt,
Then I'd go back into my warm home.
I'd find the perfect wife,
She would not lie to me.
We would have some children,
Look after them just right,
Then we would take them to school.
I would not let them go anywhere stupid.
I would not lose them because,
They would be the best children that a fish could have!

Chris Williamson (9)
Thornsett Primary School

Witches, Witches

Witches, witches cook up trouble,
Bats' wings,
Smelly socks,
Pigs' tails,
Shark skin.

Witches, witches cook up trouble,
Duck's beak,
Elephant's trunk,
Fish's skin,
Eye of newt.

Witches, witches cook up trouble,
Dog's mouth,
Panda's feet,
Tiger's claw,
Dragon's ear.

Witches, witches cook up trouble,
You're a snail,
I'm a snail,
Oh no!
Help me!

Jack Martin (8)
Thornsett Primary School

Football

Man United is my team,
Favourite, favourite, favourite team,
Win the cup,
Win the league,
Win the Premiership,
Win the shield.
Man United is my team,
Win, win, win.

Ryan Isted (7)
Thornsett Primary School

I Wish . . .

I wish I could be a chef,
As good as Jamie Oliver.

I wish I could be a racing driver,
I would win.

I wish I could be a security guard,
I would protect a crown.

I wish I could be a camera man,
I would film Harry Potter.

I wish I could be a helicopter pilot,
I would fly through fires.

I wish I could be a movie star,
I would be Jackie Chan.

Rory Marshall (7)
Thornsett Primary School

Gym

Gym is great,
Gym is good.
Lots to do,
Forwards,
Backwards,
Roll around,
Cartwheel legs off the ground,
Handstands,
Feet in the air,
Exercising,
Fantastic!
Brilliant gym.

Hannah Berry (7)
Thornsett Primary School

A Scary Dream

Going to bed at night
But in a dream
It's a dreaded sight.
You see a monster in the dark
And raiders from a lost ark.
Monsters from the deep,
Monsters that never sleep.
You get inside your bed
But you don't know
That they creep inside your head.
You get a dreaded dream,
You get outside your bed,
You look outside your window,
Eyes in a bush,
Hide under your covers
As you cover up your mush.
Finally you try to get some sleep,
But you can't stop thinking
About that monster from the deep.

Jamie Monkman (10)
Thornsett Primary School

Tracy Beaker Kenning

Curly hair,
Sly grin,
Nasty attitude,
Very cheeky.
Hates homework,
One friend,
Wicked football,
Loves dancing.
She's the best,
Tracy Beaker.

Sophie Williamson (7)
Thornsett Primary School

The Last Battle

Arrows are cocked, the walls of Minas Tirith are falling.
The Rohirrim spur their battle chargers
And raise their spears to the sky.
The Orcs prepare for the next assault,
Arrows fly, catapults fire, women and children scream.
There is an aroma of fear haunting this strong city,
This once proud city is falling to the forces of darkness,
But in the city there is hope,
A white light in the black, a wizard, a white wizard,
He stands in the courtyard protecting the white tree.
From the east comes a blue light,
Flows towards the wall,
It washes over the evil wiping all trace,
Narsil raises to the sky praising the victory.

Owen Baldwin (10)
Thornsett Primary School

Feelings By The Sea

I love the feeling of the sea,
It makes me feel full of glee.
I love the feeling of the sand
As I hold my mother's hand.
I love the feeling of the sun
As it sings its shining song.
I love to skip along the beach
And stare at the sea just out of reach.
These are my feelings
By the sea,
This is me.

Toyah Bradley (11)
Thornsett Primary School

Bats

Bats gliding through the night,
Getting ready for a fight.
Swishing and swerving through the dark
And for food they begin to mourn.
Swishing and swerving through the dark,
Their lives depending on food before dawn.

The bats fly around, starting to get worried,
Swishing and swerving through the dark.
They become dizzy,
Swishing and swerving through the dark.
Everything becomes faint and flurry,
Swishing and falling through the dark.

Iain Barr (8)
Thornsett Primary School

Seasons

All the seasons come and go,
Each one different, each one special.
Summer trees
Sway in the breeze.
Spring flowers
In meadows emerald.
Winter grass
Silver and stiff.
Autumn leaves
So crisp and fiery.
All the seasons come and go,
Each one different, each one special.

Poppy Philligreen (8)
Thornsett Primary School

If I Was Rich

If I was rich I would
Buy all the things I could.
If I was rich I would
Get my servants to clean me after I'd been in the mud.
If I was rich I would
Try and feed the poor.
If I was rich I would
Never break the law.
If I was rich I would
Buy a new car.
If I was rich I would
Go very far.

Katy Waddell (10)
Thornsett Primary School

Pets

Pets are cute.
Pets smell of the bin.
Pets are cuddly.
Pets eat all the chocolate.
Pets are fun.
Pets chew the toys.
Pets are special.
I have five,
I wish I had more,
But Mum says *no!*

Nicola Millard (8)
Thornsett Primary School

My Name Is?

My name is Daisy,
I'm awfully crazy
And funny enough I'm not that lazy.

My name is Dan,
I drive a van
And my mum always does the cancan.

My name is Ellie,
I love eating jelly
And everyone thinks I'm rather smelly.

My name is Kai,
I want to fly
Way up high like a bird in the sky.

My name is Ollie,
I have a Border collie
And I always cuddle my cute little dolly.

My name is Peter,
I can run a metre
And I can carefully pour out a litre.

My name is Ann,
I hate my gran
And you'll never guess my number 1 fan.

My name is Mick,
I'm very thick
And most of the time I feel sick.

My name is Tilly,
I'm very silly
And I always get very chilly.

My name is Tim,
I'm very thin
And I've got a girlfriend, her name is Kim.

Daisy Whewell (9)
Thornsett Primary School

Bird

If I was a bird I'd fly high in the sky,
I'd fly on people's roofs
And tweet for a pie
And then I'd call my friends
And make some dens.

Tomorrow I'd wake up,
Go to school,
Come back and play in the pool
And tomorrow I'd skive off school.

Kyle Jones
Thornsett Primary School

Weather

The weather is a mystery
Like the all-seeing eye of a cyclone.
The hail that scatters across the land, changing all to ice,
The lightning is a blinding flash that streaks across the sky.
The deafening bang of thunder,
The whiteness of snow covering all that lays before it.
The calmness of the light wind on a starry night,
The weather is a mystery.

Joe Scholes (10)
Thornsett Primary School

Stormy Weather

The stormy sky black as jet,
The stormy sky dark and wet.
The stormy sky full of gloom,
The stormy sky bringer of doom.
Thunder rumbling across the sky,
Lightning zooming by and by.
Wind ripping the leaves off the trees,
The storm is finally stopping.

Hannah Brookes (11)
Thornsett Primary School

Sunset

Sun being chased away by the moon,
Clouds and clouds of fluffy seagulls flying off to their homes,
Multicoloured blur in the sky like the wing of a Mallard
                                         glossy and glorious,
Cut out people because of the sun's rays,
Now the sun is falling, dragging minute after minute
Like a light turning off, now the sun is gone,
Dying for another night.

Jacob Walker (11)
Weston-on-Trent CE (Aided) Primary School

Steamer

Steam engine chunking with its heavy load,
70 tons of iron, steel and paint.
Gold name tab gleaming,
Hoeing ready for planting the crops corn and wheat.
Wheel turning,
Steam being thrown, heave-ho, heave-ho it cries,
Never again will it move.

Leanne Hotter (11)
Weston-on-Trent CE (Aided) Primary School

A Winter's Day

On a winter's day
I go in the bay,
I see the dew on the grass
As I tiptoe pass.

The leaves are glowing
As the winter's wind is blowing.
The sun appears round the trees,
Then I hear a buzzing bee.

Yasmyn Ford-Paulson (10)
Weston-on-Trent CE (Aided) Primary School

The Forest

Walking through the forest
I hear sounds of different pitches,
Not knowing of their maker
It sends shivers down my spine.

A group of birds launch to my right
As if disturbed by some unknown creature,
Drawing my attention with its sudden movement
I've never known such fright in any empty wood.

The trees come alive,
The creaking is their branches,
Ready to take my life it seems,
To destroy my soul also is my thought of their intention.

My heart is racing
And the feeling of the thud as I fall
Is almost a certain sign of my departure,
But it must not be - for my sense of touch still serves me.

I come around but the emptiness still lingers
With the domain of the trees,
I try to stand but it hurts,
My leg must be broken.

I seek civilisation to tend the pain of fright,
The dusk closes in on me like a trap of darkness,
I must hurry for soon it will be too dark to see,
Another sudden fright arises within me.

Thomas Hamilton (11)
Weston-on-Trent CE (Aided) Primary School

Dance Of The Rivittes

Rivittes dance in fire,
It's a strange thing to admire.
They wiggle their feet
As they gobble red meat
And then they dance their dance.

You can tell at a glance
How they love to dance.
They tap their toes,
Make sure everybody knows
And then they dance their dance.

They look very thin
And they'd fit in a pin
Though they eat lots of steak,
To tease one is a big mistake
And then they dance their dance.

Rivittes used to be jolly,
They used to like lollies
But then a storm began,
The rain poured down on man
And they danced their dance no more.

Their fire was out
And with no flames about
The Rivittes could not dance their dance,
Gleefully the lightning did prance
And they danced their dance no more.

The sea started churning,
For sun they were yearning
And then their wish came true,
The moon was new
As they danced their dance again!

Eleanor Dumbill (11)
Weston-on-Trent CE (Aided) Primary School

The Mountain

A grey giant shadowing an empty land,
He overlooks all misery and pain,
His huge boulders rumble down crushing life,
All is dark and tense.

The silence feels deadly
And the full moon looks at its own face in the black of the lake,
The cold winds chill the bone and deepen the fear.

But even as gloomy and dark as this place is
Creatures live on,
A howl,
A shriek,
A cry for help,
But no help comes and again there is silence.

I carry on and soon my blood is running cold,
With fear of something that is just about to take me,
I shiver as the darkness closes in.

I rest beneath an arm grey and cold,
It neither moves nor pulses,
I light a fire for cold and fear but nothing can banish this fright.

There is nothing and the giant stands with his burden of stone,
His feet firmly planted never to move again in this world or the next.

Douglas Brown (10)
Weston-on-Trent CE (Aided) Primary School

Reflections

It's a light maker,
Human faker,
A class spier,
Never a liar,
In different shapes or sizes,
It's you it organises,
If you're a chiller
You'll have a mirror!

Laura Poole (10)
Weston-on-Trent CE (Aided) Primary School

The Tree Of Life

It's the tree with long branches that twist and bend,
Most branches are cut but it's now on the mend.
It's an unclimbable, uncrackable, unbreakable tree,
it's the nest of the Jikobee.
At the start of spring every year the tree comes back to life,
Watch as he brings other trees back from the dead of winter.
Then he climbs the mountain,
Now listen to him roar and see him drink from the fountain.
Then he walks through to summer,
He gets a bit hot but he can survive the heat of summer.
Now he's struck by the chill of autumn,
He starts to get tired as it gets colder
But now it's winter at the end of his life.
He returns home, the other trees lose their life,
He freezes and then you can hear the return of the Jikobee.

Luke Perks (11)
Weston-on-Trent CE (Aided) Primary School

The Cat

Slyly hiding behind a tree,
Buzzing round like a bee.
Innocent through a human eye
But really that's a lie.

Blood dripping off his jaws,
Out came his sharp claws.
The blue tits flutter,
The squirrels in the trees mutter.

The fieldmice don't escape,
The poor fieldmice turn into bait.
Sniffle, snap goes the velvet cat
And all that was left was a big fat cat.

Charlotte Tyler (11)
Weston-on-Trent CE (Aided) Primary School